Team Foundation Server 2015 Customization

Take your expertise to the next level by uncovering various techniques to customize TFS 2015

Gordon Beeming

professional expertise distilled

BIRMINGHAM - MUMBAI

Team Foundation Server 2015 Customization

First published: October 2015

Production reference: 1191015

Published by Packt Publishing Ltd.
Livery Place
35 Livery Street
Birmingham B3 2PB, UK.

ISBN 978-1-78588-819-9

www.packtpub.com

Credits

Author
Gordon Beeming

Reviewers
N Satheesh Kumar
Mathias Olausson
Jim Szubryt

Acquisition Editor
Vinay Argekar

Content Development Editor
Ritika Singh

Technical Editor
Mohita Vyas

Copy Editor
Vikrant Phadke

Project Coordinator
Judie Jose

Proofreader
Safis Editing

Indexer
Tejal Daruwale Soni

Production Coordinator
Melwyn Dsa

Cover Work
Melwyn Dsa

About the Author

Gordon Beeming is an energetic and passionate person who always strives to find ways to increase and improve the productivity and friendliness of the systems he works with. He is currently a software developer and does all kinds of TFS administration, customization, and exploring as a sort of a hobby. He is part of the ALM Rangers family and has also been awarded an Microsoft ALM MVP for the past 2 years. Gordon currently works for Derivco, which is a very unique company to work for and is based in Durban, South Africa.

He has a published book to his credit, called *Team Foundation Server 2013 Customization* (`http://bit.ly/MX0yVb`). Also, as part of the ALM Rangers, he has a book to his credit, called *Managing Agile Open-Source Software Projects with Microsoft Visual Studio Online* (`http://bit.ly/1Pppi4g`).

You can find him mainly on Twitter using the handle `@GordonBeeming`, and he occasionally posts blogs at `http://binary-stuff.com/`.

I want to give a shout out to my wife and kids for their support through the late nights and sometimes sleepless nights when completing this book. Love you guys, lots!

About the Reviewers

N Satheesh Kumar holds a bachelor's degree in computer science engineering and has about 17 years of experience in software development, and project and program management. He started his career by developing software applications using Borland software products. He has worked for multiple organizations in India, the UAE, and USA. His main domain expertise is in retail, and he is currently working in Bangalore as a senior engineering manager for a top retailer in UK. Satheesh is currently managing multiple agile scrum teams to deliver the website's features. His experience also includes the implementation and customization of Microsoft Dynamics. He works with the latest Microsoft technologies and is a certified PMP (Project Management Professional).

Satheesh has also authored *LINQ Quickly*, *Software Testing using Visual Studio Team System 2008*, *Software Testing using Visual Studio 2010*, and *Software Testing using Visual Studio 2012* by Packt Publishing.

Mathias Olausson is the CTO of Solidify AB, specializing in software craftsmanship and application life cycle management. With close to 20 years of experience as a software consultant and trainer, he has worked for numerous projects and organizations, and has been very valuable when using Visual Studio as a tool to improve the way is software built. Mathias has been a Microsoft Visual Studio ALM MVP for 7 years. He is also active as a Visual Studio ALM Ranger. He is a frequent speaker on Visual Studio and Team Foundation Server at conferences and industry events, and writes blogs at `http://msmvps.com/blogs/molausson`.

He's also worked on other books such as *Pro Application Lifecycle Management with Visual Studio 2012* (`http://www.amazon.com/Application-Lifecycle-Management-Visual-Professional/dp/1430243449/`) and *Pro Team Foundation Service* (`http://www.amazon.com/gp/product/1430259957?keywords=Pro%20Team%20Foundation%20Service&qid=1444131621&ref_=sr_1_1&sr=8-1`).

Jim Szubryt has been working in the Application Life Cycle Management (ALM) space since 2006. He has been a Microsoft ALM Ranger since 2011 and a Microsoft ALM MVP since 2013, and has spoken at national conferences on ALM and DevOps topics. In his role at Accenture, he has overseen the adoption of ALM and DevOps practices. This has transformed how internal IT delivers the business goals of the $30 billion company.

Jim is an application tech arch manager in Accenture's enterprise architecture organization. His responsibilities include setting the direction for the use of dev tools, source code management, release management, and automated testing tools that support DevOps in Accenture's internal IT infrastructure. He has also worked on the book *Team Foundation Server 2013 Customization*.

Thanks to my wife, Sue, daughter, Ari, and son, Austin, for their patience with me during the summer break while I was working on this book.

---

www.PacktPub.com

Support files, eBooks, discount offers, and more

For support files and downloads related to your book, please visit www.PacktPub.com.

Did you know that Packt offers eBook versions of every book published, with PDF and ePub files available? You can upgrade to the eBook version at www.PacktPub.com and as a print book customer, you are entitled to a discount on the eBook copy. Get in touch with us at service@packtpub.com for more details.

At www.PacktPub.com, you can also read a collection of free technical articles, sign up for a range of free newsletters and receive exclusive discounts and offers on Packt books and eBooks.

https://www2.packtpub.com/books/subscription/packtlib

Do you need instant solutions to your IT questions? PacktLib is Packt's online digital book library. Here, you can search, access, and read Packt's entire library of books.

Why subscribe?

- Fully searchable across every book published by Packt
- Copy and paste, print, and bookmark content
- On demand and accessible via a web browser

Free access for Packt account holders

If you have an account with Packt at www.PacktPub.com, you can use this to access PacktLib today and view 9 entirely free books. Simply use your login credentials for immediate access.

Instant updates on new Packt books

Get notified! Find out when new books are published by following @PacktEnterprise on Twitter or the *Packt Enterprise* Facebook page.

Table of Contents

Preface

Team Foundation Server is a collaboration tool that allows you to host your source code, track requirements, tasks, testing artifacts and more, all in a single package. Integrate it with your existing IDE or editor and let your team work in a flexible environment that adapts to projects of all shapes and sizes.

From team-specific dashboards to complex server plugins, everything is covered in this concentrated guide to aid your knowledge. Delving deep, this book covers the pros and cons of check-in policies as well as their debugging and deployment strategies. After that, you will learn about Advanced XAML builds and TFS jobs. Finally, you will learn about service hooks and VSO Extensions. This will help you create new extensions and explore new levels of customization.

Explore what gives you the edge over other developers by knowing the tips and quick fixes for customizing TFS, and effectively minimize the time that users spend interacting with TFS so that they can be more productive.

What this book covers

Chapter 1, Creating a Dashboard and a Welcome Page, takes you through adding tiles, charts, and graphs to your dashboard and has a quick tour of the welcome pages.

Chapter 2, Streamlining Your Teams' Boards, helps you customize the board area of TFS, including the cards, swimlanes, and columns.

Chapter 3, Customizing Your Process Template, takes you through making modifications to the process template and shows you what type of changes you are able to make to the process template.

Chapter 4, Enhanced Work Item Forms with Field Custom Controls, talks about the pros and cons of custom controls and tells you how to create a new custom control that can be used for web and client work item forms.

Chapter 5, The Guide Standards for Check-in Policies, discusses the check-in policies in detail and what is required to make your own.

Chapter 6, Enforcing Standards with Server-side Plugins, introduces server-side plugins and what is required to make a TFS server plugin.

Chapter 7, Customizing the TFS Build, covers the customization of XAML builds and setting up builds with the new build system in TFS 2015.

Chapter 8, Creating TFS Scheduled Jobs, takes you through creating, installing, and monitoring TFS scheduled Jobs.

Chapter 9, Service Hooks, shows you what service hooks are and how you can use them to extend your TFS experience outside of TFS.

Chapter 10, VSO Extensions, gives a small example of how to create one such extension. Although this is currently only available in VSO, the same or at least very similar guidelines will be able to be applied when this is released to on-premise.

What you need for this book

You will need the following software to proceed with the examples in this book:

- Team Foundation Server 2015
- Visual Studio 2015 Community Edition or higher

Who this book is for

This book is for someone who is already familiar with TFS and is now at the point where they want to start making customizations to the way various components in TFS work. The book assumes that you know where various components in TFS are, so it won't be detailing step by step how to navigate through Team Foundation Server.

Conventions

In this book, you will find a number of text styles that distinguish between different kinds of information. Here are some examples of these styles and an explanation of their meaning.

Code words in text, database table names, folder names, filenames, file extensions, pathnames, dummy URLs, user input, and Twitter handles are shown as follows: " If you don't have a README.md file, a default markdown will show you what you might have there."

A block of code is set as follows:

```
<WebAccess version="14.0">
  <plugin name="Title Strength Indicator - Web Access"
          vendor="Gordon Beeming"
          moreinfo="https://binary-stuff.com" version="1.0">
    <modules>
      <module
      namespace="TitleStrengthIndicator.TfsTitleStrengthIndicator"
      kind="TFS.WorkItem.CustomControl"/>
    </modules>
  </plugin>
</WebAccess>
```

Any command-line input or output is written as follows:

```
copy /Y "$(TargetDir)*.*" "C:\ProgramData\Microsoft\Team Foundation\Work
Item Tracking\Custom Controls\14.0\"
```

New terms and **important words** are shown in bold. Words that you see on the screen, for example, in menus or dialog boxes, appear in the text like this: "Then, if you want to create one, you can simply click on **Edit** and then alter the markdown."

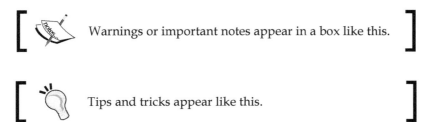

> Warnings or important notes appear in a box like this.

> Tips and tricks appear like this.

Reader feedback

Feedback from our readers is always welcome. Let us know what you think about this book—what you liked or disliked. Reader feedback is important for us as it helps us develop titles that you will really get the most out of.

To send us general feedback, simply e-mail feedback@packtpub.com, and mention the book's title in the subject of your message.

If there is a topic that you have expertise in and you are interested in either writing or contributing to a book, see our author guide at www.packtpub.com/authors.

Customer support

Now that you are the proud owner of a Packt book, we have a number of things to help you to get the most from your purchase.

Downloading the example code

You can download the example code files from your account at http://www.packtpub.com for all the Packt Publishing books you have purchased. If you purchased this book elsewhere, you can visit http://www.packtpub.com/support and register to have the files e-mailed directly to you.

Errata

Although we have taken every care to ensure the accuracy of our content, mistakes do happen. If you find a mistake in one of our books—maybe a mistake in the text or the code—we would be grateful if you could report this to us. By doing so, you can save other readers from frustration and help us improve subsequent versions of this book. If you find any errata, please report them by visiting http://www.packtpub.com/submit-errata, selecting your book, clicking on the **Errata Submission Form** link, and entering the details of your errata. Once your errata are verified, your submission will be accepted and the errata will be uploaded to our website or added to any list of existing errata under the Errata section of that title.

To view the previously submitted errata, go to https://www.packtpub.com/books/content/support and enter the name of the book in the search field. The required information will appear under the **Errata** section.

Piracy

Piracy of copyrighted material on the Internet is an ongoing problem across all media. At Packt, we take the protection of our copyright and licenses very seriously. If you come across any illegal copies of our works in any form on the Internet, please provide us with the location address or website name immediately so that we can pursue a remedy.

Please contact us at copyright@packtpub.com with a link to the suspected pirated material.

We appreciate your help in protecting our authors and our ability to bring you valuable content.

Questions

If you have a problem with any aspect of this book, you can contact us at questions@packtpub.com, and we will do our best to address the problem.

1
Creating a Dashboard and a Welcome Page

This chapter aims to guide you through creating dashboards for your team from information that exists in **Team Foundation Server** (**TFS**). We'll also take a lap around welcome pages and how they work. We will cover pinning of the following data to dashboards and how to move pinned data around on the dashboard:

- **Work item status**: Here, we'll cover the pinning of work item query counts and charts
- **Recent source code changes**: Here, we'll cover pinning a count of recent code changes
- **The build status**: Here, we'll cover pinning charts showing the build time and if they pass or fail
- **Testing charts**: Here, we'll cover pinning test related information like test status

We'll assume that you have access to TFS 2015 and have all the permissions required to create and modify various kinds of data in the team project that you are using. We'll also assume that you currently have some data that you are able to use for the samples.

What permissions do I need?

In order to pin the kind of data you want to your home page, you will need to either have **Edit project-level information** permissions for the project or be a **Team Administrator** of the team that you are trying to pin data for.

Note that if you have the **Edit collection-level information** permissions, this will not enable you to pin data to the team's home pages.

In addition to having these permissions, you will obviously need permissions to the kind of data you want to pin, for example, work item status, testing charts, and more.

What is the Team Dashboard?

The Team Dashboard is the landing page of a team. To get there, navigate to the **HOME** hub in the main navigation and then the **Overview** tab in the subnavigation. If you have a new team that has no activity yet, your dashboard will look something like this:

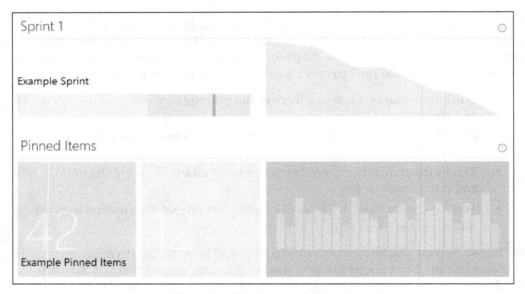

Figure 1: A default empty dashboard

The top section of the dashboard will begin to light up as your team starts work. The bottom part of the dashboard is where you can pin your own tiles for information that you may find useful for your team.

Pinning work item query data

In TFS, you are able to create queries using **Work Item Query Language** (**WIQL**) over all the work items in your team project collection. From these queries, you are able to pin some information to your dashboard to surface the results of those queries. There are two types of work item query data that you can pin to your dashboard:

- Work item query counts
- Work item query charts

Pinning work item query counts to the dashboard

Navigate to a query and click on the little arrow to the left of the query item in the query explorer. This will pop up a context menu. Click on **Pin to homepage**, as shown in this screenshot:

Figure 2: Pinning a query to the dashboard

After you have clicked on **Pin to homepage**, you will notice that the query now has a pinned icon next to it.

 This is slightly different from TFS 2013, where you would add queries to Team favorites and then that would make them show up on the team's dashboard.

Now, if you navigate back to the dashboard by clicking on **HOME** and then on **Overview** (if it is not open by default already), you will notice that there is a new tile on the dashboard for this query.

Blue tiles are for queries, and they display a count of the work items returned from a particular query. These tiles are clickable and will take you to that query in the queries tab if you click on them.

Pinning work item query charts

Before we can pin a query chart to the dashboard, we need to create the chart.

 Currently, you can only create charts for flat-list queries.

The easiest way to do this is by clicking on the tile on the dashboard from the query that we created earlier. This will take us to the query results view. Click on **Charts**, as follows:

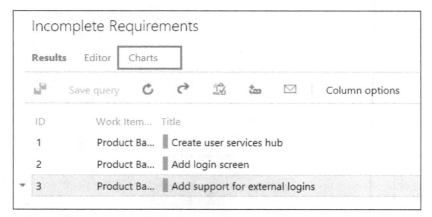

Figure 3: Query results

You will notice that by default, there are no charts for a query. To create a new chart, click on the **New Chart** button, as shown here:

Figure 4: Creating the first chart

This will open up the **CONFIGURE CHART** dialog, as shown in the following screenshot:

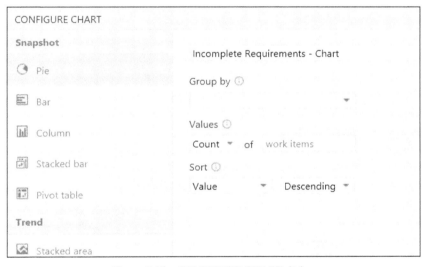

Figure 5: The CONFIGURE CHART dialog

You are able to select how the chart orders its values. Commonly, this is ordering by **Value** or **Label**. For this field I prefer using label, the main reason being that when it's pinned, it's easier to consume the information in the charts because the same *label* value appears in the same place in the chart. In the case where the chart would be consumed once off, it would be a better solution to sort by value.

The options that show up in the drop-down lists, such as **Group by** in the **Pie**, **Bar** and **Column** charts, come from the columns that are shown in your query. So, if you have a custom field, such as Department, and you want to use that field in your chart, you will need to make sure that it is visible in the query results.

For now, we have all the columns we need, so let's select **State** for **Group by**, add **by State** to our title, and then click on **OK**, like this:

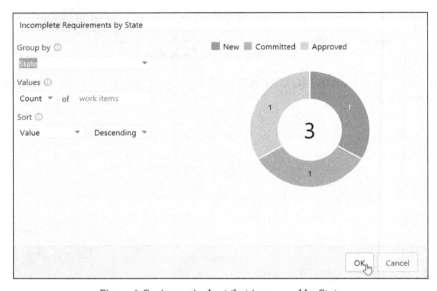

Figure 6: Saving a pie chart that is grouped by State

Now, we have created a chart and it shows as a saved chart for this query. From here, we can simply click on the ellipsis and then click on **Pin to homepage**, as shown in this screenshot:

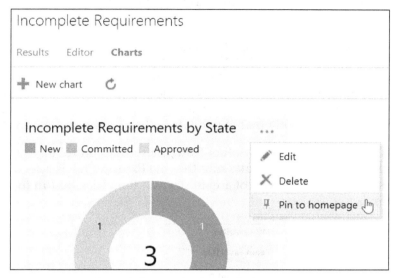

Figure 7: Pinning the chart to the home page

Visually, nothing will change on this page, letting you know that it is now on the home page. However, if you click on the ellipsis again, you will see that it now says **Unpin from homepage**, like this:

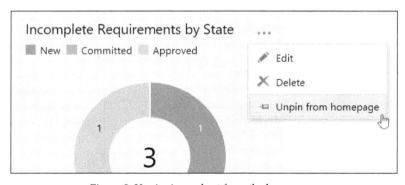

Figure 8: Unpinning a chart from the home page

If we navigate back to the home page now, we will see that our chart is visible as well.

You pinned a basic query and a basic chart to the dashboard, but you can imagine with the various chart types available how much insight this can give to a team with just a glance on their dashboard. You can get more information about charts from MSDN by going to `https://msdn.microsoft.com/Library/vs/alm/Report/charts`.

Pinning recent code changes

I've often worked in teams in which there is a component that is important to their project, such as a framework or a regulated service, and even you would find that people often keep checking the history of such a component to see whether there have been any changes recently that may not have been communicated yet.

Luckily, with TFS, you can pin any folder from the source control to your dashboard. Navigate to the **CODE** hub and make sure that the **Explorer** tab is selected. From there, click on the arrow to the left of any folder and then click on **Pin to homepage**, as shown here:

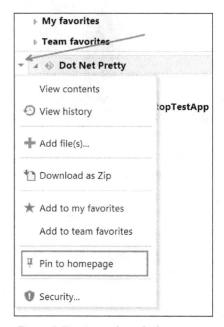

Figure 9: Pinning code to the home page

Again, you'll notice that there is a little pinned icon next to the folder that indicates that it is pinned.

Navigating back to the dashboard, you will notice a purple tile with the count of recent code changes.

You can pin any level of your source control to your home page; for example, you can pin the entire repository (as we did earlier for our Git repository), or specific folders that you care about (say, a security library folder).

Pinning the build status

With builds, we get a much nicer pinned experience—in my opinion—than with the other areas where we can pin data. Navigate to the **BUILD** hub.

Now, similarly to the recent code changes in the build explorer panel on the left, click on the arrow and then click on **Pin to homepage**, as shown here:

Figure 10: Pinning a build to the home page

As with recent code changes, this will show you a little pinned icon next to the build item.

If we navigate back to the home page, we will now see a nice tile that shows passed/failed and the duration of builds for the pinned build.

You can pin both old XAML-style builds and the new type of builds to the dashboard.

Pinning testing charts

As with work items, test suites also have charting capabilities under the **TEST** hub. Navigate to the **TEST** hub.

From here, click on the **Charts** tab of any test suite, as shown in the following screenshot:

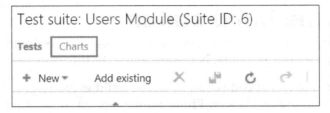

Figure 11: The Charts tab of a test suite

You will notice that for test suites, you are able to add charts that have two kinds of data sources. One type is the test case information, which is similar to the work item information but with data that is specific to test cases, and the other type is from the test case results, which give you data such as tests passed and failed.

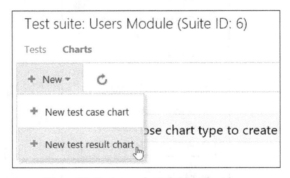

Figure 12: Test case chart data option types

We can follow the same procedure as with the work item charts to pin this; just click on the ellipsis and then on **Pin to homepage**. Again, nothing will visually tell you that this chart is pinned, but you can navigate to the home page and you will see this very chart being displayed there.

Rearranging tiles on the home page

So far, we have pinned a bunch of tiles to the dashboard and it currently looks very messy, with gaps between some of the tiles, like this:

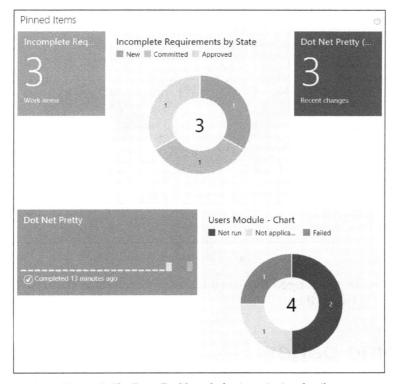

Figure 13: The Team Dashboard after just pinning the tiles

Now, obviously there is a way to rearrange these items and it is simple—just drag them around. Give it a try; drag the build tile between the work item query count and recent changes tiles, and then place the work item and testing chart next to each other.

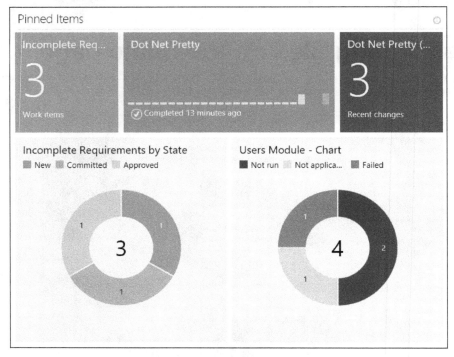

Figure 14: Pinned tiles that can be arranged

As you can see, the rearranged tiles are a lot more effective, as there isn't a bunch of white space in between them.

Welcome pages

New to TFS 2015 are welcome pages as well. If you have used GitHub before, then you'll be familiar with markdown. GitHub does a really good job at explaining all the features of markdown at `https://guides.github.com/features/mastering-markdown/`. TFS uses markdown in a couple of places, one of them being its welcome pages.

Where are the welcome pages?

The welcome pages are on the teams' home pages. You can navigate to them by clicking on the **HOME** hub and then on the **Welcome** tab.

Once you are there, you will see on the left-hand side a list of all your repos for the current team project, as shown here:

Figure 15: A list of repositories and default markdown page

If you have a README.md file in your repository, it will be displayed when you click on that repository. If you don't have a README.md file, a default markdown will show you what you might have there. Then, if you want to create one, you can simply click on **Edit** and then alter the markdown. After you have clicked on **Save**, a README.md file will be added to that repository.

Markdown files are a great way of creating documentation for your code. Some of the best reasons you'd want to do this are that it's easy to do and the markdown sits with your code, so it gets versioned with your code. This allows you to make comparisons in the documentation files as you would with any other code to see what has changed through various versions.

Summary

In this chapter, we took a lap around what can be pinned to a home page. We walked through pinning work item queries and charts created off work item queries to a home page. Then we looked at how to pin recent code changes, build statuses, and test case charts to the home page. Finally, we had a brief overview of what welcome pages are, what they are used for, and how we can use them.

In the next chapter, we'll be covering team boards in TFS and how we can customize them.

2
Streamlining Your Teams' Boards

In this chapter, we will cover the many ways in which you can customize TFS team boards. Team boards include Kanban boards, which are for portfolio-level work items (such as Epic, Feature, and Requirement), and Task boards, which are slightly less configurable at the moment, but we'll outline them as we go. With respect to these boards, we'll cover the configuration of:

- Cards
- Swimlanes
- Columns

Again, this chapter will also assume that you have all the permissions required to edit the configuration for a team as needed in the chapter examples.

Teams in TFS

Before getting started, it's worth knowing what teams in TFS are and how they are configured, as all the board settings are configured per team. Each team project in TFS is configured with a single team at its creation, named `<Team Project Name>` team. From the **Overview** tab under the team project settings, you can add more teams by clicking on **New team**, as shown here:

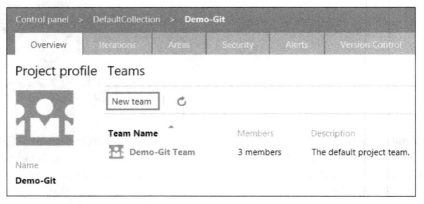

Figure 1: Team project settings

Once you have added new teams, they will appear under the team project in the **BROWSE SERVER** dialog, like this:

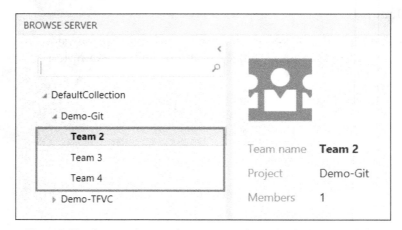

Figure 2: Newly created teams showing up in the BROWSE SERVER dialog

When you navigate to one of these projects, they will show up in the TFS web client header, as highlighted here:

Figure 3: The TFS web client selected team

Each team has its own board settings and its own pinned items for the dashboard, making it very easy and convenient to follow the common practice called "**One Team Project to rule them all**" (http://nakedalm.com/one-team-project/).

Where do I find the board settings?

If you are looking to navigate to the requirements board, you can click on the **Board** link from the team home page, or click on the **Task board** link to go to the team's current task board, as shown here:

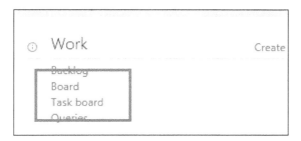

Figure 4: The Board link from the homepage

For now, let's go to the **Requirements** board. When you have navigated there, you will notice that in the top-right corner there is a settings cog icon, as shown in the following screenshot. Click on it.

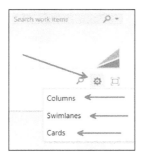

Figure 5: The settings icon on the board page

Next, you will notice that you are given three options:

- **Columns**
- **Swimlanes**
- **Cards**

If you navigate to the **Task** board and click on **Settings**, which is also found in the top-right corner, you will notice that you don't have the same options, as shown in this screenshot:

Figure 6: The settings icon on the Task board

Now that you know where the settings are, let's dive into what they do.

Configuring card settings

The card's configuration settings are identical at the moment for both kinds of boards. In TFS 2013 without any supported way to perform card customizations, many people turned to Tiago Pascoal's *Task Board Enhancer* (`http://pascoal.net/tag/task-board-enhancer/`), which added a lot of great functionality to the boards with each version. In TFS 2015, many of these features are built in and hidden under the cards configuration. Clicking on the **Cards** option under the **Settings** icon will open the **CUSTOMIZE CARDS** dialog, which looks like this:

Figure 7: The CUSTOMIZE CARDS dialog

The first thing that you'll notice along the top of the dialog is each work item type that can be made visible on this board by the current process template configuration, with bug being a special case. This is because you are able to switch them from being on the requirements or the task board using a UI switch, which can be found under the **Settings** tab. This tab is under the **Overview** tab of a TFS team, shown as follows. Note that you may have to scroll down to see the **Bugs** section.

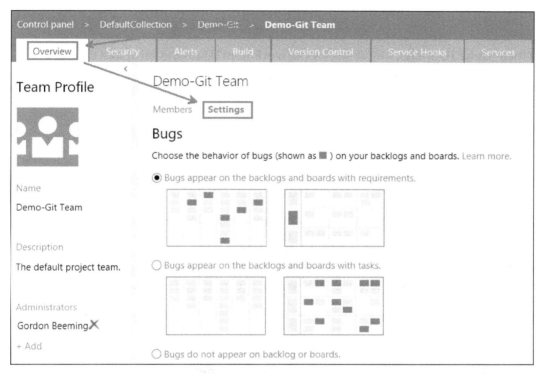

Figure 8: The team settings

For the rest of this section, we'll focus on the **Product Backlog item**, but they are mostly the same for other work item types as well. So, let's go through these settings and see what they change visually for us.

Show ID

The first option in the dialog is **Show ID**, which exists for both types of boards. This setting by default is not checked.

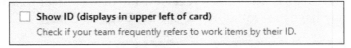

Figure 9: The Show ID option in the settings

When **Show ID** is checked, it shows the work item ID on the card, like this:

Figure 10: The work item ID showing up the work item on the board

I've noticed that this is one of the most common tasks for work items on boards. Even though lots of teams prefer to see the work item ID on the board, I have seen many teams that prefer not to show the ID, and even some teams that wish to show the ID for bugs and then not show them for requirements. Luckily, all of these scenarios are supported because each setting is configured per team per work item type.

Show Assigned To field as

The next setting in the dialog is **Show Assigned To field as**. This setting is also available on all boards. The default option here is **Avatar and full name (default)**, as shown in the following screenshot:

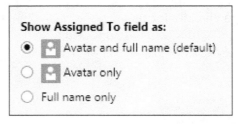

Figure 11: The Show Assigned To field as setting

This setting gives you three options: **Avatar and full name**, **Avatar only**, and **Full name only**.

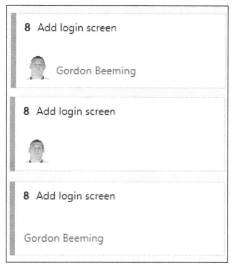

Figure 12: The Assign To setting options

I have seen that where team members have avatars set the stick to default, for other teams where they haven't added avatars to their profile, they prefer to stick to just the full name, as it was in TFS 2013. I have hardly seen any teams using the **Avatar only** option.

Show Effort

The next of the *special* configuration settings for cards is the **Show Effort** option. By default, this option is checked, as shown here:

Figure 13: The Show Effort setting

This option will show the effort on the work item. For tasks, this option is shown as **Show Remaining Work**. Talking about remaining work, it's also worth mentioning that the effort now has a similar edit experience on the board as the remaining hours did in TFS 2013.

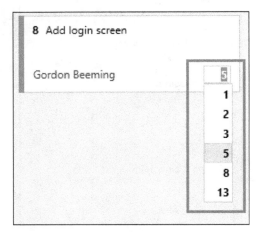

Figure 14: The effort showing on the work item with
a selectable drop-down list for effort

Previously, you would have to open the work item if you noticed that the effort was incorrect, which was slightly annoying, knowing how easy it was to adjust the remaining hours on the task board.

Show Tags

The last of the *special* field settings is for, in my opinion, one of the most powerful fields in TFS, which is the **Show Tags** option. The default here is unchecked, but I highly recommend switching this to checked if your team uses tags. If you don't use tags, switch it to true and start using them.

Figure 15: The Show Tags setting option

When enabled, your work items will get a strip under **Assigned To** and **Effort with the tags**. The first 10 tags seem to appear, and then you are presented an eleventh tag. It is an ellipsis that has the tooltip of the remaining tags.

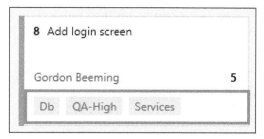

Figure 16: The tags visible on the work item

Without tags, in the past, we would basically add new fields for almost everything that we wanted to capture for a work item. Now we can tag certain work items where applicable and we can add this data into them. This saves a lot of space than if we had to add all our custom fields to the cards, as you'll see it is possible with the last configurable bit of the cards next.

Show additional fields

This last configuration option is **Show additional fields**. By default, no extra fields are shown.

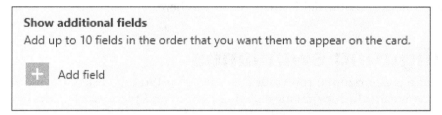

Figure 17: The Show additional fields setting

This is a great catch-all option where you would want to show any other information that doesn't have any special layout on the work item cards. Here, we can decide on adding any fields that have information about them that we would like to know by looking at the card and to find out which ones we wouldn't necessarily have to open the work item. These fields can be built-in fields or fields added through customization. Add some fields by clicking on the **Add** field. You will then notice that they are displayed on the cards as follows:

Figure 18: Showing two extra fields on the work item

If you had a customer and maybe a ticket number field on your bugs, you could show them for bugs where those fields might not make sense to show for requirements. It's also worth mentioning that the portfolio boards (Requirements, Features, and Epics) have a quick search next to the **Settings** icon. It will search for these fields, so searchable fields are great to add here.

Configuring swimlanes

A **swimlane** is a horizontal row added to your board to categorize specific work; for example, you can add a swimlane called `expedite` and place work items that are of top priority in that swimlane to visually group this higher priority work.

The next configurable bits are swimlanes. These are configurable on the Kanban board only, as it makes sense that certain tasks wouldn't go into an expedite lane; the entire requirement would move into that lane. Clicking on the **Swimlanes** option in the settings dropdown will show you the **CUSTOMIZE SWIMLANES** dialog, as shown in this screenshot:

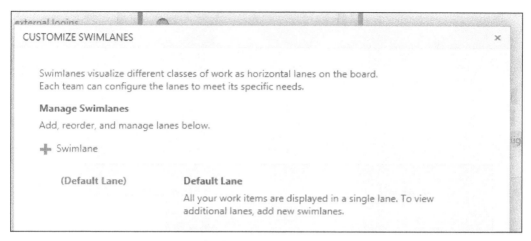

Figure 19: The CUSTOMIZE SWIMLANES dialog

To add a new swimlane, click on the add **Swimlane** button, and you'll see the following screen:

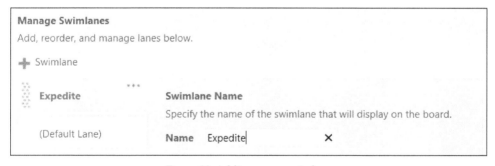

Figure 20: Adding a new swimlane

Your lane will be added with a default name, which you can and should change. You'll also notice that you can click and drag the swimlanes to reorder them vertically, and then they will be displayed in that order on the board.

Figure 21: An expedite swimlane added to the board

To remove a swimlane, make sure you have removed all the work items from that swimlane (otherwise, you'll get an error when trying to remove it). Then click on the ellipsis on the swimlane, and finally click on **Delete**, as shown here:

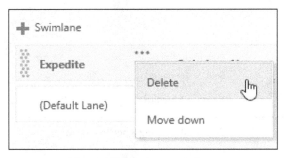

Figure 22: Deleting a swimlane

I have most commonly seen teams having only one or two extra swimlanes added, as it starts to get confusing when you have lots of swimlanes.

Configuring columns

Columns are the last configurable part of boards. These are only available with Kanban boards. The configuration here is very similar to that of swimlanes. Click on the **Columns** option in the settings drop-down list to open the **CUSTOMIZE COLUMNS** dialog, like this:

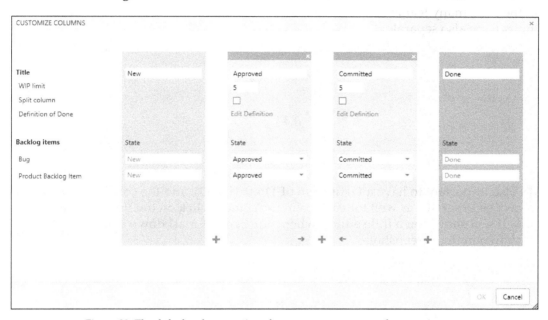

Figure 23: The default column options for a scrum process template requirement

This dialog is self-explanatory and contains most of the same functionality as in TFS 2013, with two important additions. It's on this form that we see much of the Kanban configuration occurring. From this dialog, we can rename any of the columns to be more specific to our team; for example, if it is decided that our team doesn't need the approved column, we can just click on the **x** mark in the top-right corner of the column to remove it. If we want to add a new column anywhere, we can simply click on the **+** button and add it. If we added a column in the wrong place, we can click and drag the columns to reorder them horizontally.

We can also have multiple columns that all have the same state technically; for example, we can have two **Dev** and **QA** columns and then set the **State** field for them as **Committed**. We can also set a **Work In Progress** (**WIP**) limit to a column. The new piece of functionality in this configuration dialog is the ability to split columns to have a **Doing** column and a **Done** column. Now, with this new functionality, teams are able to have one WIP limit across both their **Doing** and **Done** columns, whereas in the past, many teams added a separate column for each of these and the WIP limits were also separate.

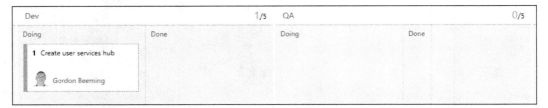

Figure 24: Split column

It's also important to have a **Definition of Done** (**DOD**), and the columns dialog allows us to set this as well for each column. You can click on the **Edit Definition** link. It will show you a little editor, where you can use markdown to set the DOD, as shown in this screenshot:

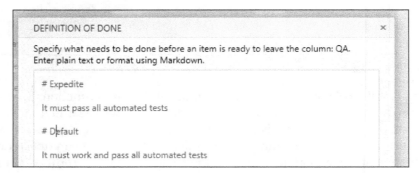

Figure 25: Editing Definition of Done

And once you have added a DOD, you will see a little information icon next to the column title. Clicking on it will show the rendered markdown, as shown in the following screenshot:

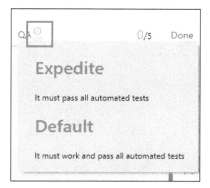

Figure 26: Viewing Definition of Done

Configuring the Kanban columns is quite powerful as it allows you to more comfortably adopt the **one team project to rule them all** concept while still letting all the teams work the way they want to.

Summary

In this chapter, we covered the different card customizations that are now available in TFS 2015 on both the Kanban and Task boards. We then looked at another feature that is new in TFS 2015—the ability to add swimlanes to the Kanban board. Finally, we looked at configuring columns on the Kanban board, which is a feature that existed in TFS 2013, but we focused on two extra features in this area that help make this board a lot more powerful.

In the next chapter, we will move on to process template configuration to perform more complex customizations.

3
Customizing Your Process Template

This chapter will assume that you have all the permissions required to perform process template customizations and upload them to your Team Projects and Team Project Collections. All the examples in this chapter are based on the scrum process template that comes out of the box with TFS 2015. We'll cover everything there is to know about customizing the process template, including the following:

- How to import and export the process template
- Best practices when customizing the process template
- What everything in the process template is
- Modifying the process template to:
  - Add a few default area paths
  - Change the test variables and configuration
  - Modify existing work item types
  - Add new work item types

- Importing and exporting specific work item tracking components

Some prerequisites

To make this chapter a lot smoother, we will skip the contents that aren't directly related to customizing the process template. The following is a list of things that you need to set up before going through this chapter so that you do not have to create them when you reach the part of the chapter that would assume that the setups already exist:

- Visual Studio 2015 should be installed and connected to TFS 2015
- You should have a local empty Git repository (it's not a requirement that this be connected to TFS)
- Your favorite XML editor; mine is Visual Studio Code (`https://code.visualstudio.com`)

What is a process template?

A **process template** is what controls about 90 percent of how your team project works in TFS. If you are spinning up a lot of Team Projects, it's a good idea to put more effort into your process template to make sure there is as little administration required as possible after you have created the team project to get things such as permissions, queries, iteration, and area paths set up.

How do I get started?

Assuming that you have made no modifications to your process template so far, you will need to download the default process template from TFS. The easiest way of doing this is by using Visual Studio. Open up Visual Studio 2015 and then navigate to **Team** | **Team Project Collection Settings** | **Process Template Manager...**, as shown in this screenshot:

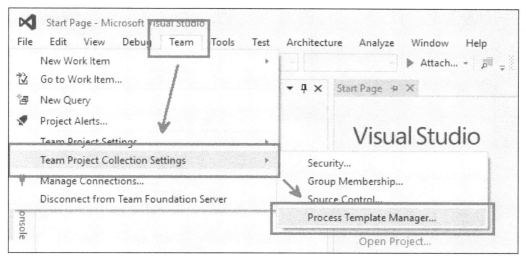

Figure 1: Opening Process Template Manager

Note that you have to be connected to your TFS Server to be able to get these options (`https://msdn.microsoft.com/en-us/library/ms181475.aspx`). You will then be shown the **Process Template Manager** dialog, make sure you have selected the **Scrum (default)** template and then click on **Download**:

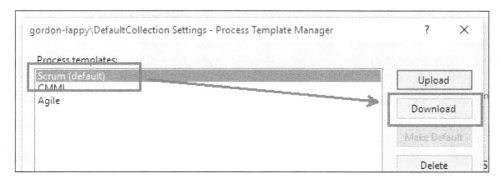

Figure 2: Downloading the process template

From here, be prompt to select a folder to save the template in. It is best practice to keep all our process template changes under the version control, so we'll save our template to a local empty Git repository, like this:

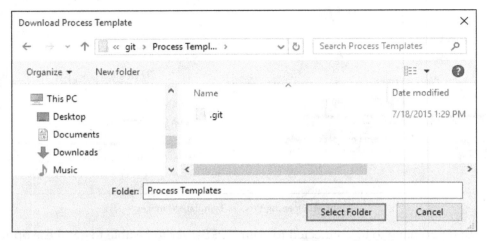

Figure 3: Saving the process template to a version-controlled folder

You will be given a message saying **Process Template downloaded successfully** when it has completed the download. Now that we have saved the files to an empty Git repository as a first step, let's commit the default process template files so that we know what changes we made along the way. Therefore, head over to the Team Explorer. The easiest way to find anything in Visual Studio is by pressing *Ctrl + Q* and typing what you are looking for. So, in this case, we'll type team explorer and then press *Enter* to select the first item in the search result, as shown here:

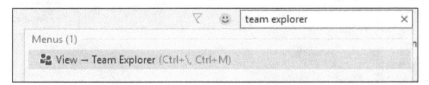

Figure 4: Opening Team Explorer using quick search

Now open up the **Changes** section by clicking on **Changes** in **Team Explorer**, like this:

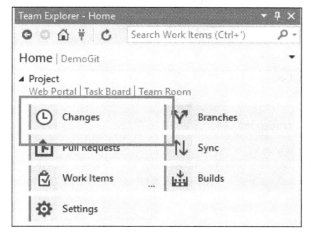

Figure 5: Opening the Changes section in Team Explorer

You will notice that by default, your files were not included in source control. Open the untracked changes files and drag the top-level folder into the **Included Changes**, as shown here:

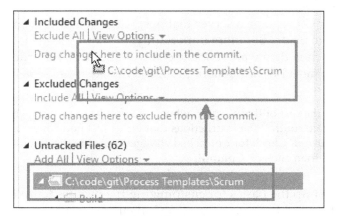

Figure 6: Adding files to source control

Now, all that is left to do is provide a commit message and click on **Commit**, as shown in the following screenshot:

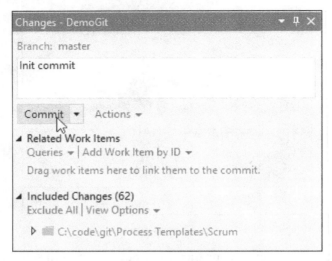

Figure 7: Committing changes to source control

You will be given a message with the commit ID and the option to sync these changes to a remote repository. For any production customizations, it's recommended that you sync/publish your Git repo on a server that hosts Git, such as TFS, so that others can see changes that are made. But more importantly, they can use the latest version of the process template when they want to make changes and not overwrite your changes because they also started with a default process template from TFS.

For the rest of this chapter, when we refer to committing changes to source control, the instructions that we've just gone over should be followed. Check for untracked changes, provide the commit message, and then click on **Commit**.

Now that we've set up the basics for customizing the process template, we are ready to start looking forward to actually carrying out customization.

The process template structure

The structure of the process template is very basic with all the top-level folders representing an area of TFS for which it has configuration and customizations. The following is a screenshot of this structure when the folder is opened in Visual Studio Code:

Figure 8: The process template filesystem structure

From the preceding structure, we will be going into various levels of detail. At a minimum we'll have an overview and, if relevant, a level where you could look into more details for them.

The root folder

There is only one file in the root of the process template by default, called `ProcessTemplate.xml`. This file is the entry point for a new team project being created. The first node is the metadata node and contains the name, description, version, and plugins that are run for project creation.

Plugins specify tasks that should be performed while creating a new Team Project in TFS. These tasks configure things such as permissions, default settings, and the default configuration.

We'll upload this template back to TFS, so let's change `name`, `description`, `type`, `guid`, and `version` to look like this:

```
<name>ScrumBut</name>
<description>This template is for teams who follow a Scrum like
framework.</description>
<version type="B7C674FA-B0F2-454A-A163-EF8F6228A7FA" major="15"
minor="0" />
```

We'll leave the plugins as they are. The next thing you'll notice in this file are the groups. All of these groups have a similar structure, as shown in the following screenshot:

```
31    <group id="WorkItemTracking" description="WorkItem definitions uploading."
32      completionMessage="Work item tracking tasks completed.">
33      <dependencies>
34        <dependency groupId="Classification" />
35        <dependency groupId="Groups" />
36      </dependencies>
37      <taskList filename="WorkItem Tracking\WorkItems.xml" />
38    </group>
```

Figure 9: The basic group XML structure

There is an ID that plugins use to know where their configuration is. The dependencies are set up so that the team project setup knows which tasks can be run in parallel, because it would just need to make sure that the group ID in the dependency has completed. Then, it can kick off that group's task. The last thing that you'll notice is that each group contains a `taskList` node. This node references the full task using the `filename` attribute, allowing `ProcessTemplate.xml` to remain cleaner. The benefits of referencing complete tasks are as follows:

- If you put your process templates under version control, having referenced tasks will lead to a lesser chance of conflicts, because other people can work in different files

- It's easier to assume what kinds of changes were made because the task files are named specifically as per the task

Commit the changes that you made with a comment such as *Updated process template name, description, and version.*

Build

The Build folder contains only one file, called Build.xml, and this file contains build permission pre-sets. So, if you have a specific TFS group that you used to always give specific permissions to for builds, after the team project creation, this is the place to give them those settings. For project-level permissions, you'll be able to define permissions for these:

- DeleteBuilds
- DestroyBuilds
- EditBuildQuality
- ManageBuildQualities
- RetainIndefinitely
- ViewBuilds
- ManageBuildQueue
- QueueBuilds
- StopBuilds
- DeleteBuildDefinition
- EditBuildDefinition
- ViewBuildDefinition
- AdministerBuildPermissions

For collection-level permissions, you'll be able to configure all the preceding permissions and also the following:

- OverrideBuildCheckInValidation

So, now that we've listed all the permissions that can be set, let's say we have a user named Bobby Green, who we wanted to be allowed to schedule builds for every team project created with our new process template. We'd have to add the following line of XML to our Build.xml file:

```
<Permission allow="ViewBuilds, ViewBuildDefinition, QueueBuilds"
identity="GORDON-LAPPY\Bobby Green" />
```

In this configuration, we are saying that for the GORDON-LAPPY\Bobby Green identity (which could have been a domain or a TFS group as well), we want to assign the ViewBuilds, ViewBuildDefinition, and QueueBuilds permissions.

Note that this will not automatically give Bobby Green access to each Team Project created with the process template. Refer to the *Groups and permissions* section for more information.

When Bobby Green is added to a team project with reader permissions, you will notice that he, instead of getting only **View build definition** and **View builds** as the default process template, gets the **Queue builds** permission as well, as shown in the following screenshot:

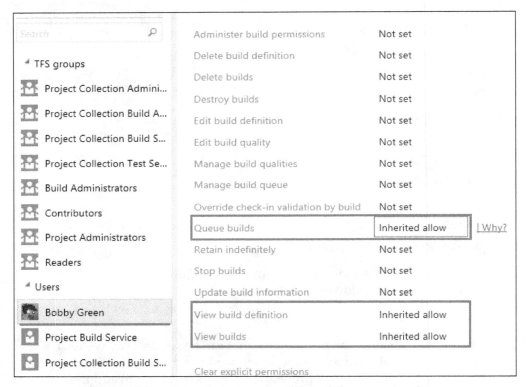

Figure 10: Permissions that were assigned through the process template

Now click on the **Why?** link for the **Queue builds** permission, which will appear when you hover next to the **Inherited allow** value, you will notice that the **TRACE PERMISSION** dialog is displayed, as follows:

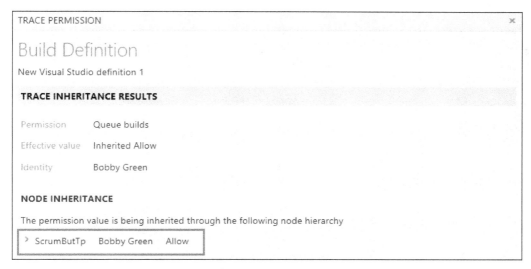

Figure 11: The TRACE PERMISSION dialog

As you can see, we are told that the reason for the permission is that from a process level, Bobby Green has permissions.

That's all for the `Build.xml` file. You can find more reference links on MSDN at `https://msdn.microsoft.com/en-us/library/dd997804(v=vs.140).aspx`.

Classification

The `Classification` folder contains two files. The first is `Classification.xml`, which contains information on what iteration and area paths should be created for the new team project. The other thing that this file has is a link to the `FieldMapping.xml` file, which has all the mapping fields used for Microsoft Project Integration. In `Classification.xml`, let's add some default area paths. To do this, you will need to consider the following area path line:

```
<Node StructureType="ProjectModelHierarchy" Name="Area" xmlns="" />
```

Replace it with a new node that contains children similar to how the iterations look in that file:

```
<Node StructureType="ProjectModelHierarchy" Name="Area" xmlns="">
  <Children>
    <Node StructureType="ProjectModelHierarchy" Name="Design"/>
```

```
        <Node StructureType="ProjectModelHierarchy" Name="Dev"/>
        <Node StructureType="ProjectModelHierarchy" Name="QA"/>
    </Children>
</Node>
```

The preceding code will add three area paths to our team project when it is created, called **Design**, **Dev**, and **QA**. When a Team Project is created with this process template, you can expect to see the following fields under the **Areas** tab under **administration**:

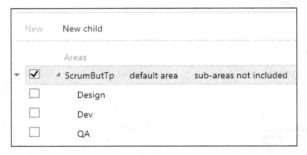

Figure 12: The area paths created from our process template

We are going to leave the `FieldMapping.xml` file alone for now, as we will not be integrating it into the Microsoft Project. Commit these changes with a comment such as *Added default area paths*.

> For more information about the `Classification.xml` file, you can go to `https://msdn.microsoft.com/en-us/library/ms243840(v=vs.140).aspx`, and to understand how `FieldMapping.xml` works, you can check out `https://msdn.microsoft.com/en-us/library/ee939346(v=vs.140).aspx`.

Groups and permissions

This folder contains a file called `GroupsAndPermissions.xml`. If you have referenced new project-level groups in any of the other task permissions' sections, such as `Build`, then this is the place to create those project-level security groups.

Earlier, we mentioned that by simply adding permissions to some permission files, users won't automatically gain access to team projects created with the process template. If you do want a user to always get access, it would be here that you give them that access. Also, it is this place where you change the default project-level permissions that users or groups have for a team project created with the process template.

Let's modify some permissions. We'll start by finding the current project readers' permission, which should look as follows:

```
<group name="Readers"
  description="Members of this group have access to the team
project.">
  <permissions>
    <permission name="GENERIC_READ"
      class="PROJECT" allow="true" />
    <permission name="VIEW_TEST_RESULTS"
      class="PROJECT" allow="true" />
    <permission name="GENERIC_READ"
      class="CSS_NODE" allow="true" />
    <permission name="WORK_ITEM_READ"
      class="CSS_NODE" allow="true" />
  </permissions>
</group>
```

We are going to change this a little. Start by adding the following XML node after the last permission node under the permissions node:

```
<permission name="WORK_ITEM_WRITE"
  class="CSS_NODE" allow="true" />
```

This will now mean that although we have a reader's permission, all users assigned to that permission will be able to save changes to work items. The other change that we are going to make is adding the following node after the permissions node:

```
<members>
  <member name="GORDON-LAPPY\Bobby Green"/>
</members>
```

This change will make sure that each new team project that is created with this process template that Bobby Green is added to the readers permission, which is now also able to write work items.

There are more details available on MSDN, where groups and permissions are covered very well, at https://msdn.microsoft.com/en-us/library/dd380669(v=vs.140).aspx.

Lab

This folder contains only a `Lab.xml` file, which is similar to `Build.xml`, and permissions for various security groups. The permissions you can set here are:

- `Read`
- `Create`
- `Write`
- `Edit`
- `Delete`
- `Start`
- `Stop`
- `Pause`
- `ManageSnapshots`
- `ManageLocation`
- `DeleteLocation`
- `ManagePermissions`
- `ManageChildPermissions`
- `ManageTestMachines`

Although the `Lab.xml` file doesn't contain any references to lab templates, if you have one, you can add it in under the `taskXml`, as follows:

```
<ProcessTemplate Type="Custom" Filename="Lab\Templates\
MyCompanyDefaultTemplate.xaml" Description="This is the default Lab
process template for My Company." ServerPath="$/$$PROJECTNAME$$/
BuildProcessTemplates" />
```

Lab templates are `.xaml` files that contain information about how you want to do some automation. An example of what you would automate with your lab template is building your application, deploying it on your lab environment, and then running a series of automated tests on the new application build.

Note how the preceding code snippet specifies where the template is on disk relative to the `ProcessTemplate.xml` file in the `root` folder using the filename. It also has a parameter attribute for where this template should be stored in the TFVC source control.

More information about `Lab.xml` can be found on MSDN at `https://msdn.microsoft.com/en-us/library/dd997893(v=vs.140).aspx`.

Reports

The reports folder contains a lot more files than we have had so far.

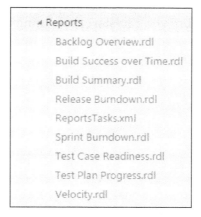

Figure 13: The Reports folder's files

The file that we are mostly going to look at here is ReportTasks.xml. The other files are all **SQL Server Reporting Services (SSRS)** report definitions, and they are referenced inside the ReportTasks.xml file. The first task in the file is for the creation of the report site for the team project, as follows:

```
3    <task id="Site" plugin="Microsoft.ProjectCreationWizard.Reporting"
4      completionMessage="Project Reporting site created.">
5      <dependencies />
6      <taskXml>
7        <ReportingServices>
8          <site>
9          </site>
10       </ReportingServices>
11     </taskXml>
12   </task>
```

Figure 14: Reports – site task

As you can see, it's rather empty and only has elements specifying that it is going to do something with a **Reporting Services** site. The other task in this file is the **Populate Reports** task. This task has all of the information required to set up the reports for your team project. It naturally has a dependency on the **Site** task because the site has to be created before you can start populating it with reports. The first node of interest in the `ReportingServices` node for this task is the creation of two folders, as shown in this screenshot:

```
19        <folders>
20            <folder path="Builds" />
21            <folder path="Tests" />
22        </folders>
```

Figure 15: Reports – creating two folders

The preceding XML specifies that two folders, called `Builds` and `Tests`, should be created. If you want to import some custom project-level reports into TFS in a folder called `Custom`, you need to specify that folder by adding another folder node, as shown here:

```
<folder path="Custom" />
```

As with `Builds` and `Tests`, this would create a new folder in the reporting services that we can save reports to. The next node specifies all the reports that should be imported. An example of one of these reports is shown as follows:

```
32    <report name="Build Summary" filename="Reports\Build Summary.rdl"
33        folder="Builds" cacheExpiration="30">
34        <parameters>
35            <parameter name="ExplicitProject" value="" />
36        </parameters>
37        <datasources>
38            <reference name="/Tfs2010ReportDS" dsname="TfsReportDS" />
39        </datasources>
40    </report>
```

Figure 16: Reports – a report node to be imported

From the report node, you can see that a name is provided—a filename that is relative to the `ProcessTemplate.xml` file. It has the information about what folder the report must be imported to (which in this case is the `Builds` folder). Lastly each report mentions the data sources that it references that need to be connected for this report definition. More information about `ReportTasks.xml` can be found on MSDN at `https://msdn.microsoft.com/en-us/library/ms243910(v=vs.140).aspx`.

Test Management

The Test Management folder also contains a lot of files.

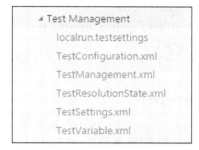

Figure 17: Test Management – the list of files

The main file here is TestManagement.xml. This time, instead of the configuration being in this file, there are four tasks that link to external files, which are TestVariable.xml, TestConfiguration.xml, TestSettings.xml, and TestResolutionState.xml.

 If you want to look up more detailed documentation for TestManagement.xml, you can go to https://msdn.microsoft.com/en-us/library/dd997878(v=vs.140).aspx.

Next, we'll briefly explain what is found in each of the files that are referenced in the TestManagement.xml file.

TestVariables.xml

In TestVariables.xml file, we'll notice that two test variables are going to be created: Operating System and Browser. Let's assume that this process template will be used only for apps that run only in the new Microsoft Edge browser. Instead of modifying the test variables for each project, we can just replace the contents of this file with the following code:

```xml
<?xml version="1.0" encoding="utf-8" ?>
<TestVariables>
  <TestVariable name="Operating System"
    description="Default operating systems">
    <AllowedValue value="Windows 10" />
  </TestVariable>
  <TestVariable name="Browser"
```

```
    description="Default browsers">
    <AllowedValue value="Microsoft Edge" />
  </TestVariable>
</TestVariables>
```

The preceding code snippet will add only a single allowed value for both the operating system and the browser, which is Microsoft Edge for the browser and because this is only available for Windows 10—that is what we will have as the OS.

TestConfiguration.xml

In this file, we'll see some test configurations. By default, it has only a Windows 8 configuration. Let's update this to have a Windows 10 configuration instead to match with the Test Variable changes we made:

```
<?xml version="1.0" encoding="utf-8" ?>
<TestConfigurations>
    <TestConfiguration name="Windows 10"
            description="Default operating system for testing"
            state="active"
            isdefault="true">
        <TestVariable name="Operating System"
            value="Windows 10" />
    </TestConfiguration>
</TestConfigurations>
```

As you can see, we specify a name for this configuration and then a Test Variable as well. We are specifying that this test configuration is for the test variable named `Operating System` and has a value of `Windows 10`.

TestSettings.xml

This file links to test settings files, by default, it is just `localrun.testsettings`. If we open `localrun.testsettings`, we'll notice that it contains some basic configuration for a basic default local test run. If you wanted to, you could change the default test run behavior. You can see that by default, the `enableDefaultDataCollectors` attribute is set to `true`, and if you change it to `false`, you can specify what data collectors you want in the `DataCollectors` node. We'll skip it for now to focus more on the TFS server and not client customization such as Microsoft Test Manager.

TestResolutionState.xml

In this file, you'll see a basic list of test resolution reasons. These are used for the reasons for which a test may have failed. You can remove some of these or add your own by adding a child node to the `TestResolutionStates` node, as follows:

```
<TestResolutionState name="Environment issue" />
```

This snippet will add the option of the environment issue for the time when we fail tests.

Commit the changes that were made with a comment such as *Change test variables and configuration to use Windows 10 and the Microsoft Edge browser.*

Version control

In this folder, we have only a `VersionControl.xml` file. It contains permissions for version control. As children of the `taskXml` node, you can specify permissions that are used for TFVC, and the permissions that you can set are the following:

- Read
- PendChange
- Checkin
- Label
- Lock
- ReviseOther
- UnlockOther
- UndoOther
- LabelOther
- AdminProjectRights
- CheckinOther
- Merge
- ManageBranch

You'll notice that in the direct child nodes of `taskXml` are two special nodes for `exclusive_checkout` and `get_latest_on_checkout`. So, you can set them for your team project instead of changing the settings after the team project has been created. The last difference that you'll notice in the child nodes of `taskXml` is that there is a Git node and under that Git node are the `server` repository default permissions for Git repositories. The permissions that you can set are:

- `GenericRead`
- `GenericContribute`
- `ForcePush`
- `Administer`
- `CreateBranch`
- `CreateTag`
- `ManageNote`

Similar to the change we made earlier, where we gave the reader permission write access, find the following node in the `VersionControl.xml` file:

```
<permission allow="Read" identity="[$$PROJECTNAME$$]\Readers" />
```

Add the `Checkin` permission to it, as follows:

```
<permission allow="Read, Checkin" identity="[$$PROJECTNAME$$]\Readers" />
```

This will now give all users who are in the readers' permission write access to the TFVC version control source code. If we want to do the same type of change for Git, we need to find the node for readers under the Git node and then add `GenericContribute` next to `GenericRead`.

Note that because Git is a distributed source control and a repository can live in TFS, GitHub, and other providers as well as local repositories, the permission that you set in this file can be enforced only when someone tries to push their commits back to TFS.

For more information about `VersionControl.xml`, visit `https://msdn.microsoft.com/en-us/library/ms243831(v=vs.140).aspx`.

Windows SharePoint Services

In this folder, there are quite a lot of files again, but as with the `Reports` folder, these are mainly just reference files that are uploaded. In this case, they are uploaded to `SharePoint`.

Figure 18: Windows SharePoint Servers – the list of files and folders

The `WssTasks.xml` file is the entry point for this folder. In it you'll notice the following code:

```
 7  <site template="Team Foundation Server Project Portal"
 8    language="1033" />
 9  <documentLibraries>
10    <documentLibrary name="Process Guidance"
11      description="How to make best use of the Team Foundation Server tools and
12      isProcessGuidance="true" />
13    <documentLibrary name="Shared Documents"
14      description="Shared Documents" />
15  </documentLibraries>
16  <folders>
17    <folder documentLibrary="Process Guidance" name="Supporting Files" />
18  </folders>
```

Figure 19: Windows SharePoint Services – the portal configuration

Here, you will see that there is a mention of the site to use. Document libraries to create and then folders to create in those document libraries. In this case, it will create only one folder called `Supporting Files` in the `Process Guidance` document library. The last thing that is in this file is a list of files that must be imported to `SharePoint`. The structure of the file node under the files is as follows:

```
<file source="Windows SharePoint Services\Process Guidance\
ProcessGuidance.html"
  documentLibrary="Process Guidance"
  target="Supporting Files/AboutWorkItems.htm" />
```

You have a `source` attribute. It is a relative path from the `ProcessTemplate.xml` file. Then you have the `documentLibrary` file to add the file to, and finally you have the target path in the document library to place the file at. All the other files that you see are reference files that are used as files to import to `SharePoint`.

WorkItem Tracking

The `WorkItem Tracking` folder is where you will probably spend most of your time while customizing the process template. `WorkItem Tracking` is one place that you will be able to make modifications to after your team project has been created, and push those updates to already created projects. There are a lot of files and folders under this folder, as shown here:

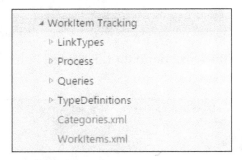

Figure 20: WorkItem Tracking – the list of files

The entry point here is the `WorkItems.xml` file. This file contains lots of links to files for **LinkTypes**, **WorkItemTypes**, **Categories**, and **ProcessConfiguration** in other folders, as you will see. It also contains permissions for **Queries**. The permissions that you can set for **Queries** include:

- `Read`
- `Contribute`
- `Delete`

- ManagePermissions
- FullControl

Let's work our way through the folders to take a look what's inside each of them. As mentioned earlier, work item tracking is one of the places that you'd want to edit once a team project has been created. And because you'd want to update all the team projects that are already using the template, we'll show you how to update them when changes are made.

Link types

While using TFS, you would have noticed specific relationships between two work items. There are a couple of link types that are embedded into TFS such as child/parent. The default process template adds three link types to your project for **SharedParameterLink**, **SharedStep**, and **TestedBy**. An example of TestedBy.xml is shown as follows:

```xml
1  <?xml version="1.0" encoding="utf-8"?>
2  <LinkTypes>
3    <LinkType ReferenceName="Microsoft.VSTS.Common.TestedBy"
4      ForwardName="Tested By"
5      ReverseName="Tests"
6      Topology="Dependency" />
7  </LinkTypes>
```

Figure 21: WorkItem Tracking – LinkTypes

As with most components, you'll find in the work item tracking section a reference name, and then there is a forward and reverse name. It describes the link for both directions like child and parent.

You can read more about link types on MSDN at https://msdn.microsoft.com/en-us/library/gg723689(v=vs.140).aspx.

Exporting and importing Link Types

You can export a link type by running the following code in a developer 2015 command prompt:

```
witadmin exportlinktype /collection:"http://gordon-lappy:8080/tfs/
DefaultCollection" /n:"Microsoft.VSTS.Common.TestedBy" /f:"c:\temp\
TestedBy.xml"
```

The `witadmin exportlinktype` tool takes in a collection parameter, an *n* (name) parameter (which is the reference name for the link type), and then an *f* (filename) parameter (this specifies where you want to save the export). To import, you have to use most of that same command with a slight change to change the command you are using from `exportlinktype` to `importlinktype`. In this case, the filename parameter refers to where you want to read the link type configuration from. So, you would use this command:

```
witadmin importlinktype /collection:"http://gordon-lappy:8080/tfs/
DefaultCollection" /f:"c:\temp\TestedBy.xml"
```

You can find more information on importing and exporting link types on MSDN at `https://msdn.microsoft.com/en-us/library/dd273716(v=vs.140).aspx`.

Queries

The `queries` folder has all the work item queries that are going to be imported into the new project under the shared queries. If you remember, when we looked at the `WorkItems.xml` file under the `QUERIES` node, alongside the permissions nodes were some Query nodes.

```
47  <QueryFolder name="Current Sprint">
48    <Query name="Open Impediments"
49      fileName="WorkItem Tracking\Queries\OpenImpediments.wiq" />
50    <Query name="Blocked Tasks"
51      fileName="WorkItem Tracking\Queries\BlockedTasks.wiq" />
52    <Query name="Work in Progress"
53      fileName="WorkItem Tracking\Queries\WorkInProgress.wiq" />
54    <Query name="Unfinished Work"
55      fileName="WorkItem Tracking\Queries\UnfinishedWork.wiq" />
56    <Query name="Test Cases"
57      fileName="WorkItem Tracking\Queries\TestCases.wiq" />
58  </QueryFolder>
59  <Query name="Feedback"
60    fileName="WorkItem Tracking\Queries\Feedback.wiq" />
```

Figure 22: WorkItem tracking – a list of queries to import

You'll see the `fileName` attribute for each of these points in the `Queries` folder. These queries are created when the new team project is created.

TypeDefinitions

This folder contains a lot of files as well, but this time, they are files that you will find yourself editing a lot. If you look at the names of the files, you'll see that they are all the work items types that are part of the Scrum template by default.

Figure 23: WorkItem Tracking – the list of work item type configurations

The basic structure of the work item type file is split into three parts:

- Fields
- Workflow
- Form

Fields

The fields section lists all the fields that are used for a specific work item.
Each `FIELD` node contains the core rules for that field. The following is an
example of one of the fields:

```
32  <FIELD name="Priority"
33        refname="Microsoft.VSTS.Common.Priority"
34        type="Integer"
35        reportable="dimension">
36    <REQUIRED />
37    <ALLOWEDVALUES>
38      <LISTITEM value="1" />
39      <LISTITEM value="2" />
40      <LISTITEM value="3" />
41      <LISTITEM value="4" />
42    </ALLOWEDVALUES>
43    <DEFAULT from="value" value="2" />
44    <HELPTEXT>Priority for completing the backlog
45  </FIELD>
```

Figure 24: WorkItem Tracking – the Priority field configuration in the Product Backlog Item

From this configuration, we can gather that this field is an integer. So, it only accepts
numeric values, only allows the values 1 through 4, and has a default value of 2.
The fields values will go through to the warehouse and also go into the cube as
a dimension. Finally, we can see that `HELPTEXT` has been provided, so this field
will have a tooltip when it's shown explaining itself. Let's add a new field for the
customer. Under the `FIELDS` node in the `ProductBacklogItem.xml` file, add the
following field:

```
<FIELD name="Customer" refname="MyCompany.Customer" type="String"
reportable="dimension" />
```

This will add a new field called `Customer` as a string for us, and it will also make
its way to the cube as a dimension. It's worth noting that fields are unique across a
team project collection, so you can't have a customer field as an integer in one team
project and have it as a string in another. Also, if you have this kind of situation,
where fields conflict across team project collections, you are going to run into some
complications when your warehouse processes. So, it's a good idea to adopt some
sort of naming standard that allows you to avoid the chance of two fields conflicting.

Workflow

The WORKFLOW section contains a list of all the states. These states contain rules that are specific to them and those rules/actions are actioned when the work item changes to that state. For example:

```
84  <STATE value="Done">
85    <FIELDS>
86      <FIELD refname="Microsoft.VSTS.Common.BusinessValue">
87        <READONLY />
88      </FIELD>
89      <FIELD refname="Microsoft.VSTS.Scheduling.Effort">
90        <READONLY />
91      </FIELD>
92    </FIELDS>
93  </STATE>
```

Figure 25: WorkItem Tracking – the state rules

The preceding screenshot shows the Done state for Product Backlog Item, and as you can see, it specifies that when the work item's state is changed to Done, the Business Value and Effort fields are READONLY. Let's add something of our own to the Done state, as follows:

```
<FIELD refname="MyCompany.Customer">
  <REQUIRED />
</FIELD>
```

This, on top of the previous rules, will also say that if we move a product backlog item to Done, then we need to have specified a Customer.

Form

The last section in the work item type file is the form. It controls the layout of the entire work item when it is shown in the web access and in client tools such as Microsoft Test Manager and Visual Studio. The XML is pretty self-explanatory, with groups, tabs, and columns making up the main layout. The columns contain one or more controls inside them, which represent the UI for the fields of the work item. Let's find the Value area field in the form layout, which would look like this:

```
<Control FieldName="Microsoft.VSTS.Common.ValueArea"
Type="FieldControl" Label="Value area" LabelPosition="Left" />
```

Then place a control under it for our customer field:

```
<Control FieldName="MyCompany.Customer" Type="FieldControl"
Label="Customer" LabelPosition="Left" />
```

When this change is pushed to an existing team project or used in a newly created team project, the control will look like what is shown in the following screenshot:

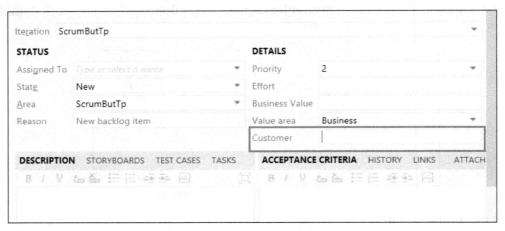

Figure 26: The new Customer field showing up on the work item form

The `FieldControl` type is a generic control type that displays each field in its own way based on the rules and the data type of a field. For example, a string field with `AllowedValues` set will show as a drop-down list where a field will be a regular textbox.

Reference links

Since work items are the most edited configuration, there are a lot of resources online where you can find more information about customizing them. The main process template link on MSDN is `https://msdn.microsoft.com/en-us/library/ aa395287(v=vs.140).aspx`. There, you will find a complete index of every XML element that can be used throughout the process template and the syntax for each.

At this point, you can commit the changes you have made with a comment such as *Added a customer field to the Product Backlog Item.*

Exporting and importing the work items

Open a Developer 2015 command prompt and run this:

```
witadmin exportwitd /collection:"http://gordon-lappy:8080/tfs/
DefaultCollection" /p:"DemoGit" /n:"Product Backlog Item" /f:"c:\temp\
ProductBacklogItem.xml"
```

The `witadmin exportwitd` tool takes in a collection parameter and then takes *p* (project name), *n* (work item name) and *f* (filename) parameters. These specify where you want to save the export. To import, you have to use most of the same command with a slight change; change the tool you using from `exportwitd` to `importwitd`. In this case, the filename parameter refers to where you want to read the work item from. You also need to remove the name (*n*) parameter, because TFS will read whatever is in your XML, or you don't have to specify the type. So, you have to use this line:

```
witadmin importwitd /collection:"http://gordon-lappy:8080/tfs/
DefaultCollection" /p:"DemoGit" /f:"c:\temp\ProductBacklogItem.xml"
```

You can find more information on importing and exporting the work items on MSDN at `https://msdn.microsoft.com/en-us/library/dd312129(v=vs.140).aspx`.

Process

In this folder you'll find the `ProcessConfiguration.xml` file, which controls what the portfolio, requirement, and task backlogs do and how they work. You'll also find information about what process template fields mean, and what core TFS field types. This information is under the `TypeFields` node, and it is how, for example, TFS knows which field requires effort in the agile process template. The type information is in a `TypeField` node, as follows:

```
<TypeField refname="Microsoft.VSTS.Scheduling.Effort" type="Effort" />
```

Downloading the example code

You can download the example code files from your account at `http://www.packtpub.com` for all the Packt Publishing books you have purchased. If you purchased this book elsewhere, you can visit `http://www.packtpub.com/support` and register to have the files e-mailed directly to you.

The next piece of configuration is the Portfolio backlogs; an example of this is as follows:

```
20  <PortfolioBacklog category="Microsoft.EpicCategory"
21    pluralName="Epics" singularName="Epic" workItemCountLimit="1000">
22    <States>
23      <State value="New" type="Proposed" />
24      <State value="In Progress" type="InProgress" />
25      <State value="Done" type="Complete" />
26    </States>
27    <Columns>
28      <Column refname="System.WorkItemType" width="100" />
29      <Column refname="System.Title" width="400" />
30      <Column refname="System.State" width="100" />
31      <Column refname="Microsoft.VSTS.Scheduling.Effort" width="50" />
32      <Column refname="Microsoft.VSTS.Common.BusinessValue" width="50" />
33      <Column refname="Microsoft.VSTS.Common.ValueArea" width="100" />
34      <Column refname="System.Tags" width="200" />
35    </Columns>
36    <AddPanel>
37      <Fields>
38        <Field refname="System.Title" />
39      </Fields>
40    </AddPanel>
41  </PortfolioBacklog>
```

Figure 27: WorkItem Tracking – the Epic Portfolio configuration

This is where you will be configuring what the `State` fields are. You also configure the `Column` fields that are shown on the backlog view by default and the fields that are shown for `AddPanel`. In the `PortfolioBacklog` node, there are attributes for what the category is; these categories can be whatever you want. You will also be specifying the singular and plural name and `workItemCountLimit`, which is the number of items that will be shown on the backlog listing for that portfolio backlog. The other attribute that isn't shown here is the parent attribute that you would see on the feature portfolio backlog item; for example, the parent value has the category of the portfolio that is its parent. The requirement and task backlogs have similar attributes as the portfolio backlogs but without the parent attribute. Then, you have `BugWorkItems`, `FeedbackRequestWorkItems`, and `FeedbackResponseWorkItems`, all of which have only the `States` information. We are also able to set `Weekends` by default for teams using this template, and we can set `WorkItemColors` for each work item. The node for a work item color is shown here:

```
128  <WorkItemColor primary="FF009CCC"
129                 secondary="FFD6ECF2"
130                 name="Product Backlog Item" />
```

Figure 28: WorkItem Tracking – the WorkItemColor configuration

Here, you can see that we specify the name of the work item type that this color configuration is for and then specify a primary and a secondary color. The primary color is the color that is shown whenever a color is shown for the work item, such as in query results and on backlog boards. Since TFS 2015 now has the more updated card styling, I don't think the secondary color is used anywhere, but for now, I'd advise using a color that is close to what you choose for the primary, maybe just a bit lighter and closer to white, like you'll see if you compare the color's for primary and secondary for any of the work item types. Now that we've explained this file a bit, let's find the **Requirements** category (`Microsoft.RequirementCategory`) and add a new column under `Column` for our `Customer` field:

```
<Column refname="MyCompany.Customer" width="400" />
```

While we are here, let's make it easy to provide a customer when creating a new requirement. Add the following snippet to the `AddPanel` function:

```
<Field refname="MyCompany.Customer" />
```

This will mean that when we are looking at the requirements backlog, we'll be able to select a customer as part of the initial work item creation instead of having to open it after creation to add a customer.

Exporting and importing the process configuration

In a Developer 2015 command shell, you can run this line:

```
witadmin exportprocessconfig /collection:"http://gordon-lappy:8080/tfs/
DefaultCollection" /p:"DemoGit" /f:"c:\temp\ProcessConfiguration.xml"
```

The `witadmin exportprocessconfig` tool takes in a collection parameter and then *p* (project name) and an *f* (filename) parameter, which specifies where you want to save the export. To import, you have to use mostly the same command, but with a slight change; change the tool you are using from `exportprocessconfig` to `importprocessconfig`. In this case, the filename parameter refers to where you want to read the process configuration from. So, you need to use this:

```
witadmin importprocessconfig /collection:"http://gordon-lappy:8080/tfs/
DefaultCollection" /p:"DemoGit" /f:"c:\temp\ProcessConfiguration.xml"
```

You can find more information about importing and exporting the process configuration on MSDN at `https://msdn.microsoft.com/en-us/library/hh500413(v=vs.140).aspx`.

Categories.xml

The `Categories.xml` file contains a list of all categories and work items that belong to those categories. It's here that you would, if you add a second work item that is also part of requirements, link that work item type to be a requirement. Or if you add a new portfolio backlog, you would come here to add the work item type you create for that backlog to that portfolio's category. An example of a category is shown in this screenshot:

```
46    <CATEGORY name="Hidden Types Category"
47            refname="Microsoft.HiddenCategory">
48      <DEFAULTWORKITEMTYPE name="Code Review Request" />
49      <WORKITEMTYPE name="Code Review Response" />
50      <WORKITEMTYPE name="Feedback Request" />
51      <WORKITEMTYPE name="Feedback Response" />
52      <WORKITEMTYPE name="Shared Steps" />
53      <WORKITEMTYPE name="Shared Parameter" />
54      <WORKITEMTYPE name="Test Plan" />
55      <WORKITEMTYPE name="Test Suite" />
56    </CATEGORY>
```

Figure 29: WorkItem Tracking – Categories

As you can see, you specify a default work item type and then any number of other work item types. You also reference the work items by their name. A single work item type can be in multiple categories, but there are some into which TFS won't let you put the same work item type; for example, you can't add a work item type as both a requirement and a task.

Exporting and importing Categories.xml

You can use the `witadmin exportcategories` tool to export your projects `Categories.xml` file. In a Developer 2015 command prompt, run the following line of code:

```
witadmin exportcategories /collection:"http://gordon-lappy:8080/tfs/
DefaultCollection" /p:"DemoGit" /f:"c:\temp\Categories.xml"
```

Again, this tool takes in a `collection` parameter and then `p` (project name) and an `f` (filename) parameter, which specifies where you want to save the export. To import, you have to use most of the same command, but with a slight change again; change the tool you are using from `exportcategories` to `importcategories`. In this case, the filename parameter refers to where you want to read the process configuration from. So, you have to use this line:

```
witadmin importcategories /collection:"http://gordon-lappy:8080/tfs/
DefaultCollection" /p:"DemoGit" /f:"c:\temp\Categories.xml"
```

You can find more information about importing and exporting categories at
`https://msdn.microsoft.com/en-us/library/dd273721(v=vs.140).aspx`.

Importing a complete process template

Now that we have gone over the full process template and made some modifications,
it would be nice to use this template. Open up Visual Studio and navigate to the
Process Template Manager. This time, click on the **Upload** button, as shown in the
following screenshot:

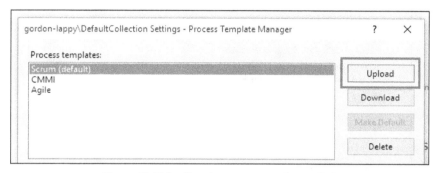

Figure 30: Uploading the process template to TFS

Then navigate to your process template and select the folder where
`ProcessTemplate.xml` is, as shown here:

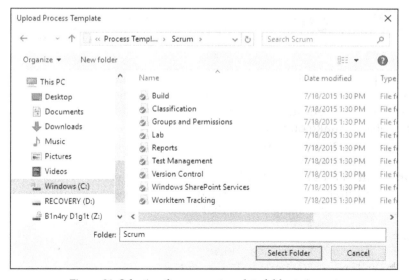

Figure 31: Selecting the process template folder to import

You'll shortly see a verifying and uploading box, and soon afterwards, a **Process Template uploaded successfully** message. You will then see your new process template in the list of process templates, like this:

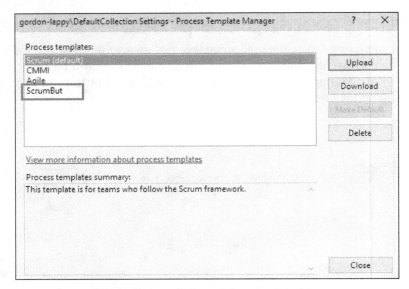

Figure 32: A newly imported process template

This process template is now ready to be used in a new team project.

Uploading changes after team project creation

As mentioned earlier, most of the time, you'll want to make modifications to your process template after the project has already been created. We showed you how to import various configuration files whenever you make changes, and that is fine when you probably make one small change and then need to upload it to only one team project. What happens if you have lots of team projects to update and you have made lots of changes? Well, for such cases, you can use a script that iterates through all the configuration files and uploads them to TFS very easily. Thus, it's a lot less manual effort and there are fewer chances of missing a customization and potentially causing errors for anyone using TFS at that time:

```
#config
$server = "gordon-lappy:8080/tfs"
$CollectionName = "DefaultCollection"
$TeamProjectNames = @("DemoGit","DemoTFVC")
```

```
$ProcessTemplateRoot = "C:\code\git\Process Templates\Scrum"
$CollectionUrl = "http://$server/$CollectionName"
$API_Version = "14.0"


#----------------------------
# don't edit below this line
#----------------------------


#get a reference to the witadmin executable path for the current api
version
$WitAdmin = "${env:ProgramFiles(x86)}\Microsoft Visual Studio $API_
Version\Common7\IDE\witadmin.exe"

#if there is a file with the name GlobalLists-ForImport.xml import it
as Global List info for the current collection
if (Test-Path "$ProcessTemplateRoot\GlobalLists-ForImport.xml")
{
    Write-Host "Importing GlobalLists-ForImport.xml"
    & $WitAdmin importgloballist /collection:$CollectionUrl
/f:"$ProcessTemplateRoot\GlobalLists-ForImport.xml"
}


#get a reference to all work item type definitions
$wit_TypeDefinitions = Get-ChildItem "$ProcessTemplateRoot\WorkItem
Tracking\TypeDefinitions\*.*" -include "*.xml"

#get a reference to all work item link types
$witd_LinkTypes = Get-ChildItem "$ProcessTemplateRoot\WorkItem
Tracking\LinkTypes\*.*" -include "*.xml"

#import each Link Type for the $CollectionName
foreach($witd_LinkType in $witd_LinkTypes)
{
    Write-Host "Importing $($witd_LinkType.Name)"
    & $WitAdmin importlinktype /collection:$CollectionUrl /f:$($witd_
LinkType.FullName)
}

foreach ($TeamProjectName in $TeamProjectNames)
{
    Write-Host "Upgrading $TeamProjectName."

    #import each Type Definition for the $TeamProjectName
    foreach($wit_TypeDefinition in $wit_TypeDefinitions)
    {
```

```
        Write-Host "Importing $($wit_TypeDefinition.Name)"
        & $WitAdmin importwitd /collection:$CollectionUrl
/p:$TeamProjectName /f:$($wit_TypeDefinition.FullName)
    }


    #import work item categories for the $TeamProjectName
    & $WitAdmin importcategories /collection:$CollectionUrl
/p:$TeamProjectName /f:"$ProcessTemplateRoot\WorkItem Tracking\
Categories.xml"


    #import work item process configuration for the $TeamProjectName
    & $WitAdmin importprocessconfig /collection:$CollectionUrl
/p:$TeamProjectName /f:"$ProcessTemplateRoot\WorkItem Tracking\
Process\ProcessConfiguration.xml"
}
Write-Host "Done upgrading team projects"
```

This PowerShell script will look through all link types, work item types, the
categories file, and the process configuration, and will update them for each team
project configured in the script for the collection that is configured. All that you have
to do is configure the settings at the top of the script, like this:

```
1    #config
2    $server = "gordon-lappy:8080/tfs"
3    $CollectionName = "DefaultCollection"
4    $TeamProjectNames = @("DemoGit","DemoTFVC")
5    $ProcessTemplateRoot = "C:\code\git\Process Templates\Scrum"
6    $CollectionUrl = "http://$server/$CollectionName"
7    $API_Version = "14.0"
```

Figure 33: The PowerShell import process template script configuration

The settings are all self-explanatory, and you'll probably need to change only the
first four.

Summary

In this chapter, we had an overview of all the pieces of configuration that make up the process template. We added a new field to an existing work item type, and then added that field to the requirements backlog columns and the add panel. We also saw how we can import and export various work item configurations using the command line.

If you would like to start slowly with editing the process template using a GUI, you can install the Power Tools, which can be found on the Visual Studio Gallery at `https://visualstudiogallery.msdn.microsoft.com/898a828a-af00-42c6-bbb2-530dc7b8f2e1`.

In the next chapter, we'll see how we can create custom work item controls for both the TFS web access and client applications such as Visual Studio and Microsoft Test Management.

4

Enhanced Work Item Forms with Field Custom Controls

In this chapter, we'll be looking at how to create custom work item tracking controls. First, we'll create a Windows form control that will be used when a work item form is displayed in a client such as Visual Studio or Microsoft Test Manager. Then, we'll create a web control that is used while displaying the work item form in the web access. We'll be covering the following topics in this chapter:

- Using a custom control in the process template
- Creating a Windows Forms Control for client applications
- Creating a web control for web access

After you've used work item tracking for a while in TFS, you can identify certain types of data that would make a lot of sense to have a slightly different control from the standard one, just to make it easier to do one or more things, such as keeping the data consistent by providing dynamic options, or maybe something as simple as a checkbox control. Now, we'll create a very simple control, which we'll call as a **title strength indicator**. It will be very similar to a password strength indicator.

As usual, we'll assume that you have all the permissions required to follow through the samples.

Prerequisites

There are two dependencies needed for this chapter. One is **Visual Studio 2015**; this can be any version, including the Visual Studio Community Edition. You will also need Fiddler for debugging web controls.

Using a custom control in the process template

Although we have not created a custom control yet, I thought it would be a good idea to start with modifying the process template to use a custom control that we will make. This will give you the extra benefit of knowing what happens if you configure a process template to use a custom control and one is not found.

Go back to where you had your process template saved (in the *How do I get started?* section of *Chapter 3, Customizing Your Process Template*) and open the `ProductBacklogItem.xml` work item definition. Find the `Title` control, which will look something like this:

```
<Control FieldName="System.Title" Type="FieldControl"
ControlFontSize="large" EmptyText="&lt;Enter title here&gt;" />
```

Now, to use a custom control (which doesn't exist yet), we will replace this line with the following code:

```
<Control FieldName="System.Title"
Type="TfsTitleStrengthIndicator" />
```

This will indicate to TFS that whenever the product backlog item is rendered, it must look for a `TfsTitleStrengthIndicator` control to use for `Title`. Update with that change using the `witadmin` tool to import a single work item, as shown in the previous chapter. At this point, you will notice that if you open a **Product Backlog Item** in Visual Studio, you receive an error message, as follows:

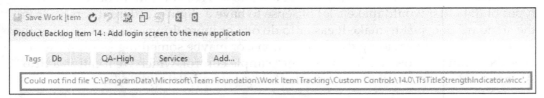

Figure 1: The client application control error for missing control

This error message is very helpful and indicates exactly where TFS is trying to read that control, which is `C:\ProgramData\Microsoft\Team Foundation\Work Item Tracking\Custom Controls\14.0\TfsTitleStrengthIndicator.wicc` in this case. You will also notice that if you navigate to this very product backlog item in the web access, you will be given a very similar error, like this:

Figure 2: The web access custom control error for the missing control

This time, we are not told exactly where TFS is trying to load the control, and for the simple reason that in the web access when we upload controls into TFS we register them with a unique name as you'll see later in this chapter, which is why this message makes sense.

This small change is all that is required to use a new custom control in a process template. Commit this change to the source control using a comment such as *adding a reference to a custom control.*

Creating a Windows Forms Control for client applications

The client control uses a standard class library with a couple of TFS assembly references, and is very lightweight.

The project setup

To start off, let's create a standard class library project. This class library can be `.net 4.5` as you need to create a library that is equal to or higher than the reference you add to it, for which our main reference will be `Microsoft.TeamFoundation.WorkItemTracking.Client.dll` in our case. This is currently at `.net 4.5`:

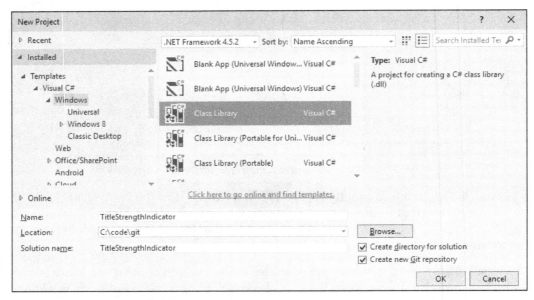

Figure 3: Creating a new class library

As you can notice, we'll place this class library in the source control as well. Next, we'll add some references. The first of the references will be to `Microsoft.TeamFoundation.WorkItemTracking.Client.dll` and `Microsoft.TeamFoundation.WorkItemTracking.Controls.dll`.

If, for some reason, you don't find one of these references, navigate to `%ProgramFiles(x86)%\Microsoft Visual Studio 14.0\Common7\IDE` in Windows Explorer and search for the assembly. In my case, I had to do this for my assembly references. Make sure you have version 14.0 of both assemblies added as it won't work if you have something else, such as 12, and you will get an error while trying to see the control, as shown here:

Figure 4: An error occurring because the referenced assembly version is incorrect

The other references that we'll need are to `System.Drawing.dll` and `System.Windows.Forms.dll`, which you should have no problem finding. Your project references should now look something like this:

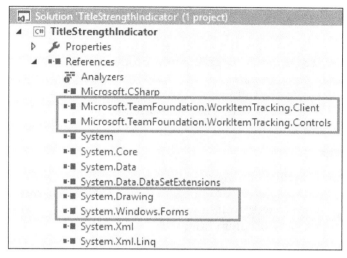

Figure 5: The project references

That's all that is required for the project setup, and you can now create your custom control.

The code for our custom client control

Now that we've added all our references, we are ready to start off with the control itself. Rename the `Class1.cs` file to `TfsTitleStrengthIndicator.cs`, and accept the message box that asks you whether you want to rename `Class1` and all its references. Next, make `TfsTitleStrengthIndicator` inherit from `System.Windows.Forms.TextBox` and `Microsoft.TeamFoundation.WorkItemTracking.Controls.IWorkItemControl`.

The first bit of code that we are going to drop in has a couple of properties, events, and a method that will be required by the `IWorkItemControl` interface:

```
public StringDictionary Properties{ get; set; }
public bool ReadOnly { get; set; }
public object WorkItemDatasource { get; set; }
public string WorkItemFieldName { get; set; }
public event EventHandler AfterUpdateDatasource;
public event EventHandler BeforeUpdateDatasource;
public void SetSite(IServiceProvider serviceProvider)
{
```

```
serviceProvider.GetService(typeof(IWorkItemControlHost));
}
```

And then add a new `using` function for:

```
using System.Collections.Specialized;
```

Let's also add a property that will make it easier to work with the `WorkItemDatasource` property by giving us a property that automatically casts the object to `Microsoft.TeamFoundation.WorkItemTracking.Client.WorkItem`. If you are not familiar with the following syntax, note that it uses one of the new C# 6, which we are now able to use with Visual Studio 2015:

```
private WorkItem WorkItemDatasourceAsWorkItem => (WorkItemDatasource
as WorkItem);
```

Now, let's get started with some logic that is specific to this control. We'll start off with the method that completes our logic as a visual indicator. This is not going to be any scientific algorithm to work out how good the title is, but rather some very basic logic off the length of the work item title:

```
public void SetIndicatorAndText(string title)
{
  if (base.Text != title)
  {
    base.Text = title;
  }
  FlushToDatasource();
  int length = title.Trim().Length;
  if (length > 25)
  {
    base.BackColor = Color.LightGreen;
  }
  else if (length > 10)
  {
    base.BackColor = Color.LightYellow;
  }
  else if (length > 0)
  {
    base.BackColor = Color.LightPink;
  }
  else
  {
    base.BackColor = Color.White;
  }
}
```

You'll have to add using to:

```
using System.Drawing;
```

Next, let's add a constructor that will listen for the TextChanged event and then call our SetIndicatorAndText method with the current Text value:

```
public TfsTitleStrengthIndicator()
{
  this.TextChanged += (sender, e) =>
  {
    SetIndicatorAndText(this.Text);
  };
}
```

Then, we are going to add the Clear method, which is called when TFS wants to clear any value for the control. For this logic, we will simply call the SetIndicatorAndText method, which we just created, passing in an empty string:

```
public void Clear()
{
  this.SetIndicatorAndText(string.Empty);
}
```

The next method that we'll implement is the FlushToDatasource method. This method is called during the save operation, although depending on how you implement your control, your data is saved as it is changed most of the time:

```
public void FlushToDatasource()
{
    if (WorkItemDatasourceAsWorkItem == null ||
        WorkItemDatasourceAsWorkItem
                .Fields[WorkItemFieldName] == null)
    {
        return;
    }
    WorkItemDatasourceAsWorkItem
                .Fields[WorkItemFieldName]
                .Value = base.Text;
}
```

Also, you have to add a using statement to:

```
using Microsoft.TeamFoundation.WorkItemTracking.Client;
```

The final method that we will implement is `InvalidateDatasource`. This method is called when the work item form tells the control to load up the current value from the work item object. We are going to ignore any state that may not have been updated in the work item up to this point, and just read the value from the work item object:

```
public void InvalidateDatasource()
{
    if (WorkItemDatasourceAsWorkItem == null ||
    WorkItemDatasourceAsWorkItem
            .Fields[WorkItemFieldName] == null ||
    WorkItemDatasourceAsWorkItem
            .Fields[WorkItemFieldName]
            .Value == null)
    {
        return;
    }
    base.Text = WorkItemDatasourceAsWorkItem
                    .Fields[WorkItemFieldName].Value
                    .ToString();
}
```

This completes all of the code that is required for any logic in our client application control. The next step is to implement the Work Item Tracking Custom Controls reference file (`.wicc`). This file contains metadata that the client work item form uses to find our control. Start by adding a new XML file named `TfsTitleStrengthIndicator.wicc`, as shown here:

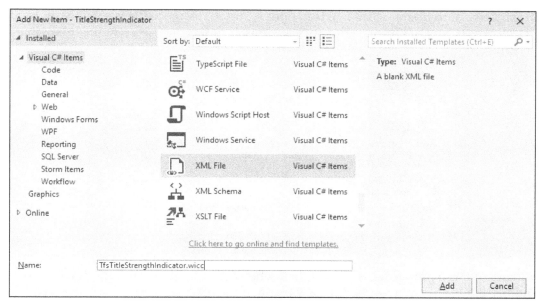

Figure 6: Adding the Work Item Tracking Custom Controls reference file

There is very little information in this file; basically, we only specify the name of the assembly that contains our control and then the full class name (including namespace) for our class:

```
<?xml version="1.0"?>
<CustomControl
  xmlns:xsi="http://www.w3.org/2001/XMLSchemainstance"
  xmlns:xsd="http://www.w3.org/2001/XMLSchema">
  <Assembly>TitleStrengthIndicator</Assembly>  <FullClassName>TitleStr
engthIndicator.TfsTitleStrengthIndicator</FullClassName>
</CustomControl>
```

Next, make sure that the **Build Action** option for the reference file is set to **None**, and also change **Copy to Output Directory** to **Copy if newer**, as shown in the following screenshot:

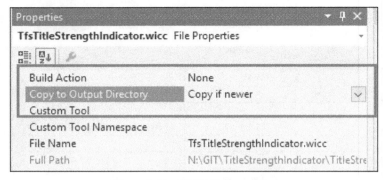

Figure 7: The WICC file properties

Changing these properties will mean that when the class library is built, it will not modify the file in any way, and if the version of the file has changed since the last build, it will be copied to the project's `bin` directory along with the project assembly (`.dll`).

We can now commit our changes to the source control.

Deploying our custom client control

Deploying the control for end users is, unfortunately, a manual process but at least a very simple one. Build your solution and then navigate to the `bin` directory of the project. From there, copy `TitleStrengthIndicator.dll` and `TfsTitleStrengthIndicator.wicc` to `C:\ProgramData\Microsoft\Team Foundation\Work Item Tracking\Custom Controls\14.0`.

This is the directory that will be scanned for custom controls. More specifically, it will be scanned for `*.wicc`, so you can place your assembly somewhere else and just have the `.wicc` file in here if you want to. If something goes wrong during the deployment for a user, they will see a message saying this:

```
Could not find file 'C:\ProgramData\Microsoft\Team Foundation\Work
Item Tracking\Custom Controls\14.0\TfsTitleStrengthIndicator.wicc'.
```

The label will still show on the form; it's just that you won't see your control. It's also a good idea to close all client apps when deploying client custom controls, but it's not a requirement to do so. If everything is working, you should be able to see that depending on what you type in the title, the background of the title field changes color. When the title contains more than 25 characters, the background will be green, as shown in this screenshot:

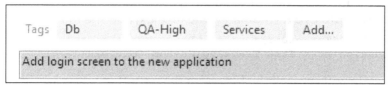

Figure 8: The indicator showing a good title

When we have 25 or fewer characters but more than 10, the background will be yellow, like this:

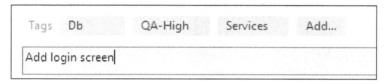

Figure 9: The indicator showing an average title

When we have fewer than 10 but more than 0 characters, the background will be red, as shown here:

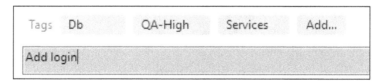

Figure 10: The indicator showing a bad title

Finally, when the title is empty, the background is white.

Debugging our custom client control

The first thing you need to do is make sure that you have opened the project in a Visual Studio that is running as administrator. The easiest way to find out whether you are running as admin is to see whether administrator is present in the Visual Studio window's title:

1. Open the project properties and navigate to the **Build Events** tab. Then, in the **Post-build event command line** textbox, add the following:

   ```
   copy /Y "$(TargetDir)*.*" "C:\ProgramData\Microsoft\Team
   Foundation\Work Item Tracking\Custom Controls\14.0\"
   ```

   This code will copy all the files from the output of your class library to the same folder where we previously copied the assemblies.

2. Next, navigate to the **Debug** tab and click on the radio button for **Start external program**.

3. Now click on the **Browse** button and find and select the Visual Studio IDE executable (`%ProgramFiles(x86)%\Microsoft Visual Studio 14.0\Common7\IDE\devenv.exe`). This means that when you run your project by pressing *F5*, Visual Studio will launch Visual Studio and attach the debugger to it.

4. Place a breakpoint in the `SetIndicatorAndText` method and then run the project by pressing *F5*.

5. Again, open a product work item that has your custom control. You'll notice that the breakpoint has been hit, proving that you can debug the code:

```
33
                 2 references | Gordon-Beeming, 17 hours ago | 1 author, 1 change
34        public void SetIndicatorAndText(string title)
35        {
36            if (base.Text != title)
37            {
38                base.Text = title;
39            }
```

Figure 11: Debugging a client custom control

You'll now be able to debug exactly as you would any other application using Visual Studio.

Creating a web control for the web access

So we've built a control for people who use Visual Studio, Microsoft Test Manager, and other client applications that show the work item form. But the web access is probably the place where your control will be used the most, so let's make it custom control.

The code for our custom control

Similar to the client control, the web control has a manifest/helper file. This time, it's named `manifest.xml`. In your same class library project, create a folder named `web` and then create the following files in it:

- `manifest.xml` (XML file)
- `TitleStrengthIndicator.TfsTitleStrengthIndicator.debug.js` (JavaScript file)
- `TitleStrengthIndicator.TfsTitleStrengthIndicator.min.js` (JavaScript file)

Note that the JavaScript files start with the full class name that was used in the client control (namespace and class name). We'll start off by adding content to our `manifest.xml` file:

```
<WebAccess version="14.0">
  <plugin name="Title Strength Indicator - Web Access"
          vendor="Gordon Beeming"
          moreinfo="https://binary-stuff.com" version="1.0">
    <modules>
      <module namespace="TitleStrengthIndicator.
TfsTitleStrengthIndicator"
              kind="TFS.WorkItem.CustomControl"/>
    </modules>
  </plugin>
</WebAccess>
```

In our manifest, we put some information. TFS uses it to display the extension in the web access. Then we specify the namespace, which has the same value as what is in the `.wicc` file as `FullClassName`. Next, let's place the following in our `debug.js` file:

```
TFS.module("TitleStrengthIndicator.TfsTitleStrengthIndicator",
[
"TFS.WorkItemTracking.Controls",
```

```
    "TFS.WorkItemTracking"
], function () {
  var witOM = TFS.WorkItemTracking;
  var witControls = TFS.WorkItemTracking.Controls;
  function TfsTitleStrengthIndicator(container,
                                     options,
                                     workItemType) {
    this.baseConstructor.call(this,
                              container,
                              options,
      workItemType);
  }
  TfsTitleStrengthIndicator.inherit(witControls.WorkItemControl, {

    // Code that is like the client code

  });
  witControls.registerWorkItemControl("TfsTitleStrengthIndicator",
TfsTitleStrengthIndicator);
  return { TfsTitleStrengthIndicator: TfsTitleStrengthIndicator };
});
```

The preceding code snippet loads our control as a module using the same namespace that is in our manifest, and then the other important thing it does is register the TfsTitleStrengthIndicator control.

It also sets up the local variables to the work item tracking reference and implements the control inheritance for us. That is all what you would mostly have in most of these types of controls obviously, just changing the namespace and class name.

The next code snippet—if you look at it carefully—is exactly our client controls logic, but in JavaScript:

```
_control: null,
setIndicatorAndText: function (title) {
  if (this._control.val() != title)
  {
    this._control.val(title)
  }
  this._getField().setValue(title);
  var length = title.length;
  if (length > 25)
  {
    this._control.css('background-color', "#90EE90");
  }
```

```
    else if (length > 10)
    {
      this._control.css('background-color', "#FFFFE0");
    }
    else if (length > 0)
    {
      this._control.css('background-color', "#FFB6C1");
    }
    else
    {
      this._control.css('background-color', "white");
    }
  },
  clear: function () {
    this.setIndicatorAndText("");
  },
  invalidate: function (flushing) {
    this.setIndicatorAndText(this._getField().getValue());
  },
  _init: function () {
    this._base();
    this._control = $("<input type='text' value=''
style='width:100%'/>").appendTo(this._container);
    var that = this;
    this._control.change(function () {
      that.setIndicatorAndText(that._control.val());
    });
    this._control.keyup(function () {
      that.setIndicatorAndText(that._control.val());
    });
  }
```

Note that we have the same `setIndicatorAndText` method and it does the same thing. We have the `invalidate` and `clear` methods as well. This is a very simple control, and that's why the logic looks so similar in the client and web controls. Often in the real world, these look very different from each other because the controls are a lot more complex.

Commit all of these changes with a message such as *Adding the web custom control*.

Deploying our custom control

Let's see what we need to do to deploy our custom control:

1. Firstly, zip up the three files for your control and navigate to the TFS home page. Then click on **Administer Server** in the top-right corner.

2. We then click on the **Extensions** tab. Next, click on **Install**.

3. Now click on the **Browse** button, navigate to and select the ZIP file that you just made, and click on **OK**. You will be shown the extension with all the metadata that you put into the manifest file, as shown in the following screenshot:

Figure 12: The web custom control uploaded

4. All that's left to do is enable our control by clicking on **Enable**.

Now, if you were to browse to a work item in the web client, you would notice the same behavior as what you saw in Visual Studio for our Title field.

Debugging our custom control

Even though it's just a couple of steps, if you had to perform those steps every time you made a small modification to see whether your changes worked, it would take forever to complete a single plugin. Also, it would be very hard to debug, because the cycles between making a change and being able to test them are too far apart.

Enabling TFS debug mode

Enabling debug mode in TFS will make all the scripts that TFS uses decompressed so that you are able to read them and try debugging your extension a lot more easily. To enable debug mode, navigate to the server root URL and append _diagnostics to it, so you will get something like http://gordon-lappy:8080/tfs/_diagnostics. Then click on the **Disabled** link next to **Script Debug Mode:**. You are now able to step through your code with your browser's built-in *F12* tools as you would any other JavaScript.

Configuring Fiddler – an AutoResponder rule

Fiddler has a really cool feature that allows you to respond to requests with static files in your PC. This is one of the most useful tools for helping you debug your TFS plugins:

1. Open **Fiddler** and then open the **AutoResponder** tab.

2. Check **Enable automatic responses**, and also check **Unmatched requests passthrough**.

3. Next, click on **Add rule**. Then, in the **Rule Editor** tab (at the bottom of the screen), enter the following `regex` pattern in the top textbox `regex:http://.+/_plugins/.+/TitleStrengthIndicator. TfsTitleStrengthIndicator.js`.

4. Next, in the response (bottom textbox), place the full path to the `debug.js` file in your project.

5. Finally, add the same `regex` pattern, but this time, put the response as `header:CachControl=no-cache`.

Your auto responder should look something like this:

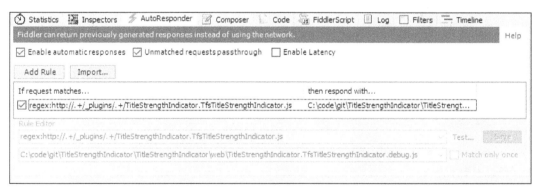

Figure 13: AutoResponder configured in Fiddler

Now you'll notice that you can make any changes you want in the `debug.js` file, and they will be picked up straightaway after a page refresh. When you are ready to share your plugin updates, zip it up and upload it on TFS for others to use.

Summary

In this chapter, we looked at how to create a custom client control that gets used in applications such as Visual Studio when a work item form that is expected to render our control is shown. We also saw how we can debug client controls and enable debug mode for TFS web access.

In the next chapter, we are going to take a look at how we can reinforce best practices with check-in policies.

5
The Guide Standards for Check-in Policies

In this chapter, we are going to cover the creation of a custom check-in policy. We'll go through the following high-level topics:

- Implementation — what it takes to write the code
- Deployment — what is required to get this to your end user
- Useful policies — policies already created by the community

Check-in policies are very useful as you can make sure that certain requirements are met before a check is made that might not be meeting some standards. In my opinion, it's one of the easier customizations to perform. It's also important to mention that check-in policies are currently only supported by TFVC.

Prerequisites

There is one additional dependency for this chapter besides TFS 2015 — Visual Studio 2015. This can be any version, including the Visual Studio Community Edition.

The project setup

The first thing that you'll need to create in a check-in policy is a new **Class Library** project. Let's call it **BigChangesPolicy**:

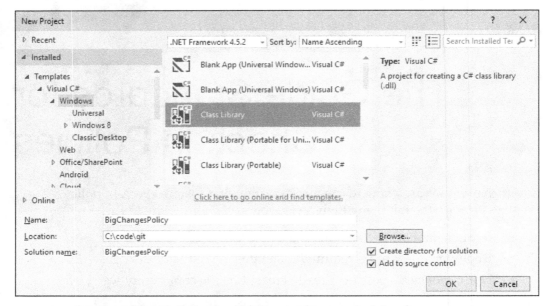

Figure 1: A new class library project for a new check-in policy

Then, the only reference you need is `Microsoft.TeamFoundation.VersionControl.Client.dll`, which you can find in your assemblies list. But if you don't—for some reason—then, as before, navigate to `C:\Program Files (x86)\Microsoft Visual Studio 14.0\Common7\IDE` and search `Microsoft.TeamFoundation.VersionControl.Client.dll`.

Even though we don't really need it, let's add a reference to System.Windows.Forms.dll so that we can use the MessageBox class. Let's rename Class1.cs to BigChangesCheckInPolicy.cs. At this point, our project should look like what is shown in the following screenshot:

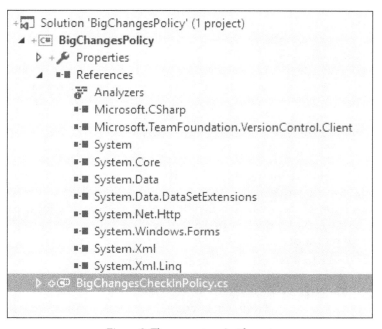

Figure 2: The current project layout

That's all that is required for the project setup.

Implementation

The code for a check-in policy is really simple:

1. First, make the BigChangesCheckInPolicy class inherit from PolicyBase:

   ```
   public class BigChangesCheckInPolicy : PolicyBase
   {
   }
   ```

2. You will also need to add the following using statement:

   ```
   using Microsoft.TeamFoundation.VersionControl.Client;
   ```

3. Now, we'll implement the methods that are required by the abstract methods in `PolicyBase`. Let's first use the following code to describe our policy:

```
public override string Description =>
        "The Big Changes Checkin Policy makes sure that if you "+
        "make lots of changes you are adding a work item to "+
        "the check-in";
public override string Type =>
        "Big Changes Checkin Policy [Dialog Box]";
public override string TypeDescription =>
        "The Big Changes Checkin Policy makes sure that if you " +
        "make lots of changes you are adding a work item to " +
        "the check-in [Dialog Box]";
public override bool Edit(IPolicyEditArgs policyEditArgs) =>
            true;
```

4. We added some string methods describing our extension for various places in Visual Studio, such as the `Policies` dialog, and then we returned a true value for `Edit`, because we aren't going to have any logic to run on policy editing. Now, the last piece that we need for a check-in policy is the `Evaluate` method:

```
public override PolicyFailure[] Evaluate()
{
  int filesWorkOn =
    PendingCheckin.PendingChanges.CheckedPendingChanges.Length;
  int workItemsLinked = PendingCheckin.WorkItems.CheckedWorkItems.
Length;
  if (filesWorkOn >= 5 &&
        workItemsLinked == 0)
  {
    return new PolicyFailure[]
    {
new PolicyFailure("Big Changes require linked work items", this)
    };
  }
  else { return new PolicyFailure[0]; }
}
```

5. So, the logic that we have included basically checks whether five or more files have been modified and then, if we have no work items linked, the policy will fail with the `Big Changes require linked work items` message. The step that is required to get this check-in policy to work is adding the `Serializable` attribute to the class:

```
[Serializable]
```

6. Our policy is "code complete", but there are two methods and a property that I find are quite handy to override as well to provide a better user experience. The first of these methods is the `Activate` method:

```
public override void Activate(PolicyFailure failure)
{
   MessageBox.Show("Activate method.",
      "How to fix your policy failure");
}
```

7. For now, we will just pop up a message showing that we are in the `Activate` method. So, when our check-in policy is installed and shows the policy warning, if you double click anywhere on the message, it will pop up run into this method:

Figure 3: The Activate method

8. At this point, it might be helpful to explain why the policy warning has been thrown. So maybe in this case, we would mention the files that have changed, or at least some of them, and explain that because there is no work item linked, the policy has failed. The next method which is a nice to override is the `DisplayHelp` method:

```
public override void DisplayHelp(PolicyFailure failure)
{
   MessageBox.Show("Help method.",
      "Prompt Policy Help");
}
```

9. Then add the following `using` statement:

```
using System.Windows.Forms;
```

10. Again, for now, we'll show a message. This method is called when the **Help** in the warning message is called, as follows:

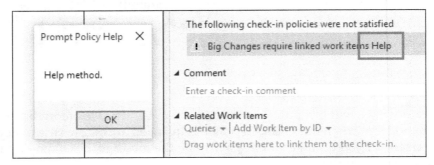

Figure 4: The Display Help method

11. At this stage, it would be helpful to pop up or open some documentation so that the developer can better understand the reason for the policy breach. The last helpful item to be overridden is the `InstallationInstructions` property:

```
public override string InstallationInstructions =>
    @"Run ""\\GORDON-LAPPY\CompanyCheckinPolicies\install.bat"" " +
    "as Administer to install this check-in policy";
```

12. This property adds a little extra information to the end of the default message that is displayed to a user who is missing the check-in policy from their machine:

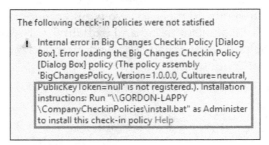

Figure 5: The installation instructions message

This could be very useful if there is an open source project in which a check-in policy is used, or for new developers working on a project so that they know where to install bits from instead of having to ask other developers.

Deploying a check-in policy

The deployment is also really simple and basically requires just a single registry addition. Open `regedit.exe` and navigate to `HKEY_CURRENT_USER\SOFTWARE\Microsoft\VisualStudio\14.0\TeamFoundation\SourceControl`. In this key, you will need to add a new key named **Checkin Policies**, and in that key, you will have to create a new string value. The string value name needs to be the value of your project's output assembly, which in the case of the sample code is **BigChangesPolicy**. Then, you need to set the value of this string to the full path to your assembly, which will be the full path to `BigChangesPolicy.dll` in the case of the sample. This should look something like what is shown in the following screenshot:

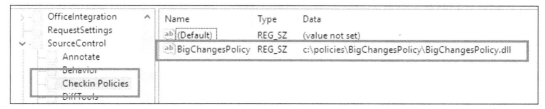

Figure 6: The registry entries for a check-in policy

On the left, you can see the **Checkin Policies** key that we added, and then we have the string value pointing to our policy in the panel on the right.

Configuring a check-in policy to be used

To configure your check-in policy, open up a Visual Studio instance, connect to a TFS TFVC (Team Foundation Version Control) Team Project, and navigate to **Team menu | Team Project Settings | Source Control...**, as shown here:

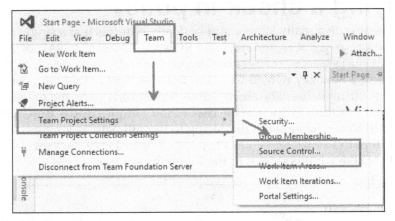

Figure 7: Opening the source control options

This will open the **Source Control Settings** dialog. Click on the **Check-in Policy** tab, and then click on **Add...**, like this:

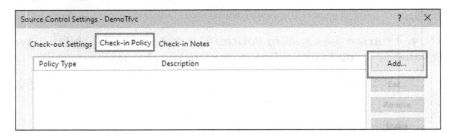

Figure 8: The Source Control Settings dialog

This will open the **Add Check-in Policy** dialog. You'll notice here that the Type function that we specified in our code is shown in the listing, and when we click on it, the TypeDescription value is shown in the description at the bottom of the dialog. Click on the newly added check-in policy and then click on **OK**, as shown in the following screenshot:

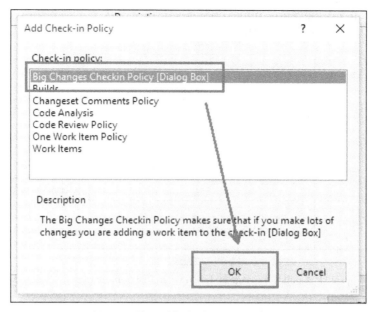

Figure 9: The Add Check-in Policy dialog

Now you have to return to the **Source Control Settings** dialog, where you will see the policy reflecting in the list. Click on **OK** to apply these changes, as shown in this screenshot:

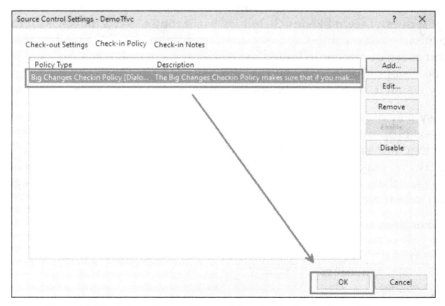

Figure 10: Check-in policy – adding and showing in Source Control Settings

Now, if we open a project and make changes to five files, we'll be shown a warning when we go to the **Pending Changes** window, like this:

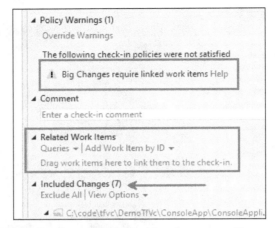

Figure 11: A policy message is shown when five or more files are changed

As you can see in the preceding screenshot, we have seven changes included in the check-in and no work items linked, so the policy warning is shown.

Deploying to the masses

The preceding deployment method is all that you need to get the check-in policy working. It doesn't seem like much, but it's frustrating to get a message saying that you are missing some components required to check some code in. Now, if we were to request every developer to build the code on their machine and then follow the deployment steps shown, or even copy the compiled bits from somewhere and then manually install it, there would be some problems.

So, an easy way of making this a slightly easier experience is by using the installation instructions property as we did and then pointing the user to an install directory. Let's put together a small installer that we can use. The first thing we will do is go to the registry and export the registry settings for the check-in policy key so that we can get a .reg file that can be run by us and can add the entries back into the registry, or at least update them. You should see something like this:

```
Windows Registry Editor Version 5.00

[HKEY_CURRENT_USER\SOFTWARE\Microsoft\VisualStudio\14.0\
TeamFoundation\SourceControl\Checkin Policies]
"BigChangesPolicy"="c:\\policies\\BigChangesPolicy\\BigChangesPolicy.
dll"
```

Update the path you see in your `.reg` file to be the same as `c:\\policies\\` `BigChangesPolicy\\BigChangesPolicy.dll`. Then add that `.reg` file to your check-in policy project and rename it to `CheckInPolicy.reg`. The next step is to add a new `.bat` file to our project, called `install.bat`. In it, we'll place the following code:

```
@ECHO OFF
cd /d c:\
md policies
cd policies
md BigChangesPolicy
xcopy /Y /s "%~dp0\*.*" "c:\policies\BigChangesPolicy"
regedit.exe /s "C:\policies\BigChangesPolicy\CheckInPolicy.reg"
pause
```

What this code does is start off by creating a folder called `policies` in the `C:` drive. Then it creates a `BigChangesPolicy` folder inside that. Next, it copies all the files from some UNC share. For the purpose of this sample, I have shared my `Debug` folder called as `CompanyCheckinPolicies`, and as mentioned in our sample code's installation instructions, the user can navigate to `\\GORDON-LAPPY\` `CompanyCheckinPolicies\install.bat` to install the check-in policy. Change **Build Action** to **None** for both the `.reg` file and the `.bat` file that you added to the project, and also change **Copy to Output Directory** to **Copy if newer**. Build the project. Then you can either navigate to the `Debug` folder and run `install.bat`, or share that folder as we did for the sample and test `install.bat` from there. After running the install, you will see that the check-in policy still works, and if you were to run it on other developers' machines, it would work for them as well. Although this is still a bit of a manual process, I use it because if you are a big company, there is a good chance that your IT department has software that is capable of pushing registry keys out to your machine, and also pushing files out to your machine. So, what you can do if this is the case for you, is ask them to automatically push out a copy of some UNC path and the registry value to the machine of each user who has Visual Studio installed. Then, your deployment is taken care of.

Now, what if everyone on the project is not working in the same organization, or the IT department is not able or willing to do this type of deployment for you? Well, that's where you'd use the more traditional ways of getting extensions and plugins into a developer's Visual Studio instance. You create an extension and publish it on either an internal share to install from or the Visual Studio Gallery.

A great post on packaging check-in policies was written by Terje Sandstrom more than 3 years ago, and I still use it as an outline today. It can be found at `http://geekswithblogs.net/terje/archive/2012/03/10/packaging-custom-checkin-policies-for-visual-studio-using-vsix.aspx`.

Existing check-in policies

In this section, I thought I'd share with you some check-in policies that many people use today and aren't out of the box, rather than cover any more examples.

Colin's ALM check-in policies – VS 2015 and VSO

The first check-in policy that's definitely worth looking at is one from Colin Dembovsky. This policy allows you to make sure that code reviews are performed before a check-in is allowed. This can be found in the Visual Studio Gallery at `https://visualstudiogallery.msdn.microsoft.com/045730ee-63c0-498e-b972-42b05a2d0857`. You can also find the code for it on GitHub, which is extremely useful because, for one, you can see how the policy was written. Furthermore, you can add to it and submit pull requests if you have useful features to add, and these can be found at `https://github.com/colindembovsky/ColinsALMCornerCheckinPolicies`.

Microsoft Visual Studio Team Foundation Server Power Tools

The next is one from Microsoft, and it is TFS Power Tools. It contains a couple of check-in policies. You can get the extension at `https://visualstudiogallery.msdn.microsoft.com/898a828a-af00-42c6-bbb2-530dc7b8f2e1`. These tools contain the following extensions:

- **Custom Path Policy**: This policy scopes other policies to specific folders or file types
- **Forbidden Patterns Policy**: This policy prevents users from checking in files with forbidden filename patterns

- **Work Item Query Policy**: This policy allows you to specify a work item query whose results will be the only legal work items for a check-in to be associated with

This tool also has other non-check-in policy components that you can use when customizing TFS.

Summary

In this chapter, we took a look at how to create a check-in policy that is based on the current pending changes changed files count, we showed a policy warning requiring a work item be added to the check-in. We then looked at ways to install and deploy a check-in policy, and also took a look at some policies that we can download and install instead of reinventing the wheel.

Check-in policies can be overridden, as you probably know, so in the next chapter, we are going to look at server-side plugins and how we can use them to enforce certain policies so that they can't be overridden.

6
Enforcing Standards with Server-Side Plugins

Server plugins are extremely useful for validating changes such as code check-ins and work item changes performed without having to deploy extensions to all users of team projects that require logic.

In this chapter, we will be looking at what server plugins are and how we can use them to enforce standards. The topics that we will cover include the following:

- Differences between check-in policies and server plugins, including their pros and cons
- Creating a server plugin that executes on code check-in and saved work items
- Deploying a server plugin
- Debugging a server plugin

Check-in policies versus server plugins

Check-in policies, as we just saw (in *Chapter 5*, *The Guide Standards for Check-in Policies*), run completely on the client. This allows us to provide a nicer user experience, because validation is done on the client, whereas server plugins run completely on the server. Therefore, we can't launch any kind of UI on the server and rather have to rely on only sending helpful messages when validation fails.

You are able to override a check-in policy warning and proceed with a commit against any policies that are setup for the team project, whereas server plugins have no way to override unless you build logic into them that only validates on certain types of data making them ideal for when you need to enforce some behavior.

With check-in policies running on the client, the computing resources for whatever operations are required run on the client. On the other hand, with server plugins, all of the logic is executed as part of the overall request to TFS. So, if you have code that is bloated, you will slow down user experience for all users and potentially require more hardware to deal with the extra load that is added from running the plugins.

Server plugins are easier to deploy because it's done by dropping the plugin assemblies into a folder on the server, which is much easier than check-in policies. The latter need to be deployed to each user that requires them.

> However, with easy deployment comes a major downside. When you deploy a server plugin, the IIS application pool that TFS runs under is recycled, causing any requests currently being made to TFS to fail or run slowly until the application starts up again.

If your plugin is simple and lightweight, then I'd say that it is a good candidate for a server plugin. If you have an idea of a plugin that is more complicated or has a UI to help a user fix the issues for which validation fails, then that would be a good candidate for a check-in policy.

> It's also worth noting that other types of server plugins do exist. One of the more common types is `WorkItemChangedEvent`, which executes when any field is changed for any work item.

As you can see, there are a lot of pros and cons to both server plugins and check-in policies, and it ultimately depends on what kind of customization you need to implement for the path that you will take.

The project setup

The aim of this plugin will be to enforce the logic that we created in *Chapter 5, The Guide Standards for Check-in Policies*, with our check-in policy, instead of having it optional by allowing users to override it.

As usual, we'll start with checking the minimum requirements before you start implementing your own custom logic. Start off by creating a **Class Library** project, as shown here:

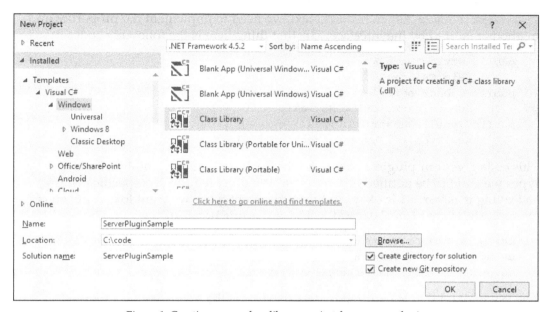

Figure 1: Creating a new class library project for a server plugin

Add references to the following `.dll` files, all of which can be found on the TFS application tier server at the `C:\Program Files\Microsoft Team Foundation Server 14.0\Application Tier\Web Services\bin` path:

- `Microsoft.TeamFoundation.Common.dll`

- `Microsoft.TeamFoundation.Client.dll`

- `Microsoft.TeamFoundation.VersionControl.Client.dll`

- `Microsoft.TeamFoundation.WorkItemTracking.Client.dll`

- `Microsoft.TeamFoundation.WorkItemTracking.Server.dll`

- `Microsoft.TeamFoundation.Framework.Server.dll`

- `Microsoft.TeamFoundation.VersionControl.Server.dll`

That's all that is required for creating our server plugins. However, before we continue, let's rename the `Class1.cs` file in our project to `BigChangesServerPlugin.cs`.

The basics of server plugin code

The first thing that we need to do for a server plugin is make our class, which in this case is `BigChangesServerplugin`, inherited from `Microsoft.TeamFoundation.Framework.Server.ISubscriber`. Next, we need to implement the properties and methods required by the interface. The first thing here is the following code:

```
public string Name =>
        "Big Changes Server Plugin";
public SubscriberPriority Priority =>
        SubscriberPriority.Normal;
public Type[] SubscribedTypes() =>
        new Type[] { typeof(CheckinNotification) };
```

This code gives our plugin a name and the execution priority and lists what types we want to be notified on events for. We don't require any specific priority, so leaving it as `Normal` is okay, and then the event types we want to execute on is `CheckinNotification`. Also add a new `using` function for:

```
using Microsoft.TeamFoundation.Framework.Server;
using Microsoft.TeamFoundation.Common;
using Microsoft.TeamFoundation.VersionControl.Server;
```

The last method that is required by the interface is the `ProcessEvent` method:

```
public EventNotificationStatus ProcessEvent(
  TeamFoundationRequestContext requestContext,
  NotificationType notificationType,
  object notificationEventArgs,
  out int statusCode,
  out string statusMessage,
  out ExceptionPropertyCollection properties)
{
  throw new NotImplementedException();
}
```

This is the method that is called on every request that is made to TFS that is first of all the plugins that you specified and then has also made it through for all the other server plugins that have a priority higher than your plugin. The `requestContext` parameter contains all of the information for the current request, for example, what the team project is.

The notificationType function can have two values:

- DecisionPoint, which is called when you are able to make a decision to influence the request status. Not every type of event calls the server plugin for a decision point.

- The other option is Notification, which every event type will be called for, and in notifications, you are not able to influence the outcome of the request.

The notificationEventArgs function contains event-specific information; for example, for a work item changed event, it will contain what that work item is and what was modified as part of the request. The statusCode function, statusMessage function, and the properties are all used to determine the success or failure of the execution of the server plugin, as well as the meta information to be passed to the caller who made the request to help understand why, for example, the request would not succeed.

Solution attempt 1 – use event type DecisionPoint

Let's add some logic to the body of our ProcessEvent method. The first thing that we'll do is satisfy the out parameters with this code:

```
statusCode = 0;
statusMessage = string.Empty;
properties = null;
```

The next thing that we'll want to do is add a try catch method in case anything unexpected happens during our plugin execution:

```
try
{
  // logic goes here
  return EventNotificationStatus.ActionPermitted;
}
catch (Exception ex)
{
  statusCode = -1;
  statusMessage = "[Error] " + Name + ", error details: "
  + ex.ToString();
  EventLog.WriteEntry("TFS Service",
    statusMessage, EventLogEntryType.Error);
  return EventNotificationStatus.ActionDenied;
}
```

In this catch block, you have to determine whether you want your plugin to pass or fail if there is an exception during execution. In this sample, we are saying that if something breaks, we want to deny the current action. However, we could change the return status to `ActionPermitted`—as we did in the `try` block—if we wanted to allow requests that fail our plugin. You will also require this `using` statement:

```
using System.Diagnostics;
```

Inside the `try` block, we are going to place the following code:

```
if (notificationType == NotificationType.DecisionPoint &&
   notificationEventArgs is CheckinNotification)
{
  CheckinNotification args =
            notificationEventArgs as CheckinNotification;
  if (args.GetSubmittedItems(requestContext).Count() >= 5)
  {
    var tfsTPC =
      TfsTeamProjectCollectionFactory.GetTeamProjectCollection(
        new Uri("http://localhost:8080/tfs"));
    var vcs = tfsTPC.GetService<VersionControlServer>();
    var changeSet = vcs.GetChangeset(args.Changeset);
    if (changeSet.WorkItems.Length == 0)
    {
      statusMessage = "Big Changes require linked work items.";
      return EventNotificationStatus.ActionDenied;
    }
  }
}
```

The preceding code will require these `using` statements:

```
using Microsoft.TeamFoundation.Client;
using Microsoft.TeamFoundation.VersionControl.Client;
```

The code starts off by checking whether the current execution is for a decision point request and that `notificationEventArgs` is a `CheckinNotification`, which it should be, because that is the only type that we have requested to be executed. We then check how many files were submitted for this check-in:

- If there are five or more files, we proceed to make a new request to the version control to check which work items are linked to the change set that we are given as part of the request

- If none are linked, we will set `statusMessage` and return an `ActionDenied` status

So, if you follow the steps for deploying a *server plugin* section that follows, you will notice that this code doesn't work. Instead, you will get a major error, as shown in this screenshot:

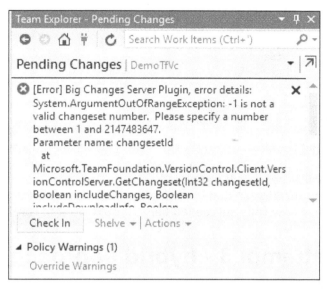

Figure 2: Exception in the server plugin

The error message comes from our `catch` block and says that a change set number can't be `-1`. This code should work, however, if the change set number passed is valid. The reason for using `-1` is that we are still in the decision point execution, so a change set has not been created yet.

Solution attempt 2 – use event type notification

So, it seems obvious that we should try changing the code just inside our `try` block to check for `DecisionPoint` to be checking for `Notification`, as follows:

```
if (notificationType == NotificationType.Notification &&
    notificationEventArgs is CheckinNotification)
```

Well! When you run this, you will see that your execution makes it all the way to the `ActionDenied` returned status this time:

```
49              var vcs = tfsTPC.GetService<VersionControlServer>();
50              var changeSet = vcs.GetChangeset(args.Changeset);
51              if (changeSet.WorkItems.Length == 0)
52              {
53                  statusMessage = "Big Changes require linked work items.";
54                  return EventNotificationStatus.ActionDenied;  ≤1ms elapsed
55              }
56          }
```

Figure 3: Debugger showing that we've reached the ActionDenied status return

But you'll notice that the check-in is still successful. So, in this case, what is happening is that because we are in the `Notification` execution, TFS doesn't care what status code we return. This is because it has already committed any necessary changes and is just showing a notification so that you trigger some other event if you need to know that the check-in has now fully succeeded before you'd want to continue.

Solution attempt 3 - hybrid approach, validate the policy

Before we continue here, let's say that that TFS did provide us with `changeSetId` so that the first attempt worked or that in the notification attempt, that TFS would roll back the change if we said it has a status of `ActionDenied`. There was a lot of overhead for each request there. We checked the submitted items, which was fairly light, but then we called into the version control source to get that `changeset` in order to see what work items were linked to it.

All of this adds up and makes your TFS experience a lot slower. This is a very simple scenario of how something that feels like a quick and easy plugin can affect request times for where your plugin is installed. Also, most likely when you do use TFS server plugins, they will be a lot more complicated compared to this.

So now that we've gone over all this, what would be the correct way to validate that if 5 items are checked in that a work item is also linked? Well, you remember that we made that check-in policy, right? One of the values that is passed to us as part of the request, is what the overrides were for the check-in and what the policy failure messages were.

So, we can take out all of the code that is inside our `try` block and replace it with the following code:

```
if (notificationType == NotificationType.DecisionPoint &&
  notificationEventArgs is CheckinNotification)
{
  CheckinNotification args =
              notificationEventArgs as CheckinNotification;
  var ourPolicy = args.PolicyOverrideInfo.
    PolicyFailures.FirstOrDefault(o => o.PolicyName ==
                      "Big Changes Checkin Policy [Dialog Box]");
  if (ourPolicy != null)
  {
statusCode = -1;
    statusMessage = ourPolicy.Message;
    return EventNotificationStatus.ActionDenied;
  }
}

  return EventNotificationStatus.ActionPermitted;
```

We will still check whether we have the correct event `args` and whether we are in a `DecisionPoint` execution, as we've seen that being in the `Notification` execution is of no help to us. This is because we want to be able to cancel the check-in. We will then attempt to get a policy from the policy override that matches our policy name. Next, if we find an override for our policy, we will set the status message to the message that was set by our policy and return `ActionDenied`.

So, if we deploy the code again and override the policy, we would now get an error, as follows:

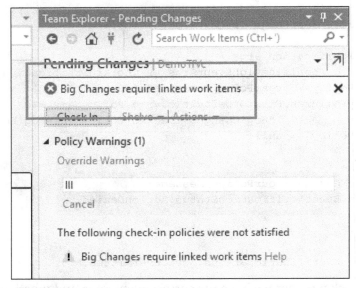

Figure 4: A server plugin throwing an error as expected

Now, we get the error that matches the warning thrown by the policy. With this approach, you provide the user with a good experience because if it is a big check-in, they won't have to wait for all the files to be sent to the server, and then our method executes and the check-in is simply blocked. Instead, they will be told straightaway by the check-in policy that they need that work item. Then, when they don't provide it, we can just enforce that policy by completely blocking all requests that have not met the policy requirements.

Deploying a server plugin

Deployment is really easy, as mentioned before. All that you need to do is copy your project assembly and any of its dependencies that are not TFS-related assemblies to `C:\Program Files\Microsoft Team Foundation Server 14.0\Application Tier\Web Services\bin\Plugins` in the TFS Application Tiers. So, in the case of the current sample, these would be only `ServerPluginSample.dll` and `ServerPluginSample.pdb`.

As a reminder, when you do this step, the TFS application pool will be recycled, causing possible performance issues and potentially data loss issues because of failed requests.

That's all that is required to deploy a TFS server plugin.

Debugging server plugins

In order to debug server plugins, you will need to make sure that there are remote debugging tools installed on the TFS Application Tier. You can read more about remote debugging at `https://msdn.microsoft.com/en-us/library/y7f5zaaa(v=vs.140).aspx`. If you have TFS installed locally — which is best practice because then changing the binaries does not impact other users — then you won't require remote tools.

 It is strongly advised that you do not attach to a production TFS Application Tier, as you will be blocked of requests while you debug and will also be adding extra overhead to the server while debugging.

If TFS is on the same machine as you are running Visual Studio on, then you must be running Visual Studio as Administrator in order to debug a site in IIS. Open the **Debug** menu and then click on **Attach to process...**, as shown here:

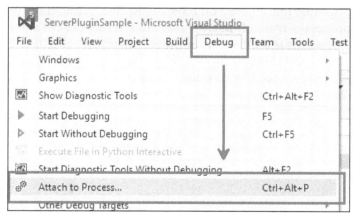

Figure 5: Visual Studio – Attach to Process

This will open up the **Attach to process** dialog, as shown in the following screenshot:

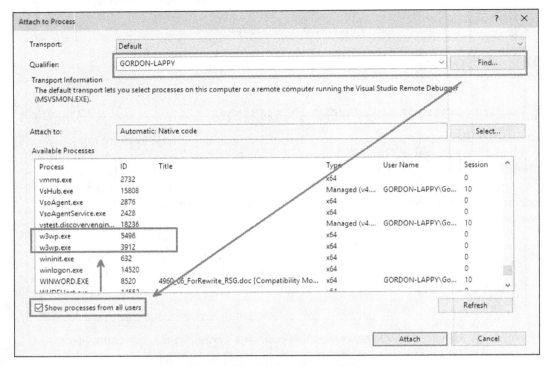

Figure 6: The Attach to Process dialog

In this dialog, you must make sure you have connected to the TFS Application Tier, click on **Show processes from all users** if it is not already ticked, and then find the w3wp.exe process, which is an IIS worker process that runs TFS. If you attached to the correct w3wp.exe process, you should see some time after loading symbols that your Visual Studio shows your breakpoints lit up.

This indicates that the symbols for your project are loaded, and you can debug your server plugin just as you would debug any other project's code:

```
                    0 references | 0 changes | 0 authors, 0 changes
     24             public EventNotificationStatus ProcessEvent(
     25                 TeamFoundationRequestContext requestContext,
     26                 NotificationType notificationType,
     27                 object notificationEventArgs,
     28                 out int statusCode,
     29                 out string statusMessage,
     30     ☐           out ExceptionPropertyCollection properties)
     31             {
     32
  ●  33                 statusCode = 0;
     34                 statusMessage = string.Empty;
     35                 properties = null;
     36
     37                 try
```

Figure 7: Debugging a server plugin

That's all for debugging server plugins. Every bit of the debugging experience here is the same as the debugging of any other web application.

A slightly more complicated example

We have looked at a basic plugin and have discussed how to keep our server plugins as light as possible. Well, this sample is not completely lightweight, but it does give TFVC uses. This is something cool that exists for Git users because of the nature of distributed source control which is auto-linked to Git. It commits to work items just by adding #id to your commit message.

This makes it easier to link your changesets to work items if you are used to the Git way of doing it, or maybe if you use a tool such as git-tf, which allows you to use Git commands against TFS by translating all server commands into TFVC commands and doing some fancy work behind the scenes so that you feel as if you are using Git. But actually, you are using TFVC.

So, we'll set up all of the code the same way as before, but this time, we will call the GitStyleWorkItemLinkingServerPlugin class. All that we are going to change in the opening properties is the name, to Git Style Work Item Linking Server Plugin. In our try block, we will be looking for a notification. This is because we want to know what the change set number is:

```
if (notificationType == NotificationType.Notification &&
    notificationEventArgs is CheckinNotification)
```

Then, inside this `if` statement, replace the code with what is shown here:

```
CheckinNotification args =
    notificationEventArgs as CheckinNotification;
TfsTeamProjectCollection tfsTPC = null;
VersionControlServer vcs = null;
WorkItemStore wis = null;
foreach (Match match in Regex.Matches((args.Comment ?? string.Empty),
@"#\d{1,}"))
{
  if (tfsTPC ==null)
  {
    tfsTPC =
      TfsTeamProjectCollectionFactory.GetTeamProjectCollection(
        new Uri("http://localhost:8080/tfs"));
    vcs = tfsTPC.GetService<VersionControlServer>();
    wis = tfsTPC.GetService<WorkItemStore>();
  }
  Changeset changeset = vcs.GetChangeset(args.Changeset);
  int workItemId = Convert.ToInt32(match.Value.TrimStart('#'));
  var workItem = wis.GetWorkItem(workItemId);
  if (workItem != null)
  {
    //now create the link
    ExternalLink changesetLink = new ExternalLink(
        wis.RegisteredLinkTypes[ArtifactLinkIds.Changeset],
        changeset.ArtifactUri.AbsoluteUri);
    //you should verify if such a link already exists
    if (!workItem.Links.OfType<ExternalLink>()
        .Any(l => l.LinkedArtifactUri == changeset.ArtifactUri.
AbsoluteUri))
    {
      changesetLink.Comment = $"Change set '{args.Changeset}'" +
                   " auto linked by a server plugin";
      workItem.Links.Add(changesetLink);
      workItem.Save();
    }
  }
}
```

You'll also need to add using:

```
using System.Diagnostics;
using System.Text.RegularExpressions;
using Microsoft.TeamFoundation.WorkItemTracking.Client;
```

```
using Microsoft.TeamFoundation;
using Changeset = Microsoft.TeamFoundation.VersionControl.Client.
Changeset;
using Microsoft.TeamFoundation.Framework.Server;
using Microsoft.TeamFoundation.VersionControl.Server;
using Microsoft.TeamFoundation.Common;
using Microsoft.TeamFoundation.Client;
using Microsoft.TeamFoundation.VersionControl.Client;
```

What this code does is as follows: it starts off by using a regex expression over the comment of the check-in to look for the #id pattern. Next, for each pattern that it finds, it tries to find a TFS work item with that ID and then links the change set number to that work item ID.

So, suppose you now create a check-in and have no work item linked to that check-in. Then, directly after the check-in, if you click on the change set link at the top of Team Eexplorer, it will load up that change set's details, and you'll see that it now knows that it is linked to a work item:

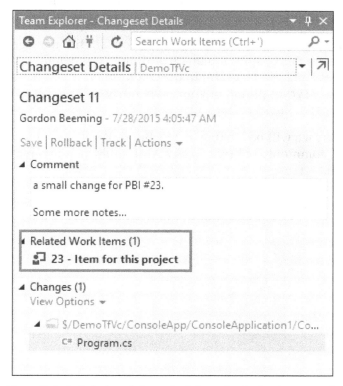

Figure 8: Auto-linked work items check-ins using hashes in comments

This is a great example showing how you can use the notification execution path to trigger some other behavior in TFS. A plugin like this one allows a developer to speak fluently in their comment as they are probably already doing. Then, because links are virtually present in the comment already, we let TFS link to work items for us.

 Using this approach would mean that if you have the policy to require work items on check-ins enabled, users would basically have to override the policy on every check-in.

This is a good example of an awesome piece of functionality that cannot fit into your environment because of some other factors, such as the required work item check-in policy.

Summary

In this chapter, we looked at server plugins, comparing them to check-in policies, creating our own plugins, and deploying and debugging server plugins.

At the time of writing this book, there is a project on GitHub that contains samples similar to the ones in this chapter. I plan on adding to it when there are interesting server plugins that I feel can be useful to the community. If you have an idea or want to contribute a server plugin of your own, navigate to `https://github.com/Gordon-Beeming/TFS.ServerPlugins`.

In the next chapter, we will be looking at TFS Build. We'll cover the old-style build definitions, commonly referred to as XAML builds, and then look at the new build system.

7
Customizing the TFS Build

In this chapter, we will be looking at the build system in TFS. We will start off by looking at the XAML build system, and then take a look at the new build system that has been released with TFS 2015. We'll cover these topics:

- What is an XAML build template?
- Creating custom activities
- Adding a custom activity to your build activity
- A walkthrough of the new build system

For our XAML build sample, we will be creating a build activity that generates some very basic documentation. We will store our code samples in a Git repository, but will be building a project that resides in TFVC.

The prerequisites

The sample will use the **Calc Api** project from GitHub as a target solution to build, which you can find at `https://github.com/Gordon-Beeming/CalcApi`. Download this code from GitHub or from the source provided with this book, and then add the code to a TFVC team project.

What is an XAML build template?

A TFS XAML build template is a XAML file that contains all the information on how a build should behave when run. XAML looks like XML and is currently, commonly used for WPF, Silverlight, and Universal Applications; where it is used to describe how the UI works, which is different from how it is used in TFS.

Build definitions use build templates. These definitions contain all the metadata, such as selected code paths, build arguments, and any other information that the build template has made available for use by the build definition.

Should I use the old or the new build system?

So, now that we have two supported build systems in TFS, a question that often arises is, "Which one should be used?" Lots of people who have been using TFS for years have put a lot of investment into the build workflows, infrastructure, and customizations, so it doesn't make sense that they switch all their workloads to the new system. I would advise using the new build system going forward as it promises to provide more flexibility, as you will see in this chapter.

How do I download a build template?

XAML build templates are used to create a part of your TFVC source control, and if you've upgraded from previous versions of TFS, you will still have the definitions in source control although the XAML definitions are not stored in the source control as of TFS 2013.

We need to download the XAML template from TFS so that we are able to make modifications to it that are specific to the tasks we require to be run at build time.

Therefore, to get a copy of the default templates, you need to start executing the following steps to create a new build in order to download the template:

1. Let's open **Visual Studio**. Then, in **Team Explorer**, open up the **Builds** page.
2. Next, click on **XAML Build Definitions** to open that section. Then, click on **New Build Definition**, as shown here:

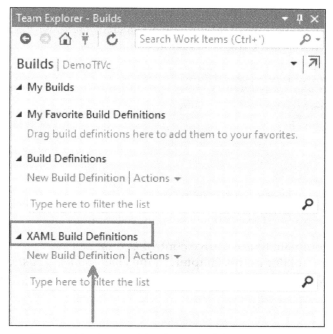

Figure 1: The New Build Definition link in Team Explorer

This will open up the build definition configuration window. We aren't going to create a build at this point; we just came here to obtain the template.

3. Click on the **Process** tab and then on the **Show details** extender control, like this:

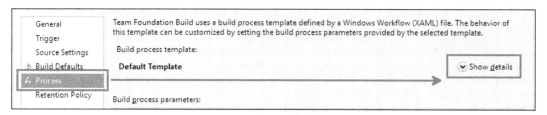

Figure 2: Opening the build definition process template

4. You will now be shown an option to change the Build process file, which by default lets you choose a TFVC project from the following:

   ○ `TfvcTemplate.12.xaml`

   ○ `UpgradeTemplate.xaml`

   ○ `LabDefaultTemplate.11.xaml`

5. We are going to add to the default build template, which is `TfvcTemplate.12.xaml`, so we make sure that template is selected. Then, we click on **Download**, as shown in the following screenshot:

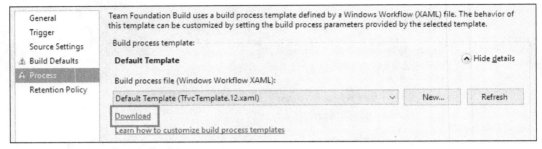

Figure 3: Downloading the build template

6. Save the template to the source control as `CustomTfvcTemplate.12.xaml`. We will use it later in this chapter, in the *How do I use a custom activity in a build template?* section.

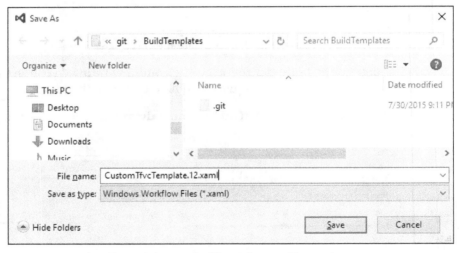

Figure 4: Saving a build template to a Git repository

Now that we have downloaded the template, we can move on to create a build using it, and then we'll make customizations to that build template.

How do I create a new build?

We have downloaded and added the default TFVC build template to the source control, so we can now create our new build upfront. Then, as we change the template, we can just run new builds to see the changes in action.

 At this point, I'm expecting that you are connected to TFVC on a team project where you have checked in the Calc Api project mentioned earlier in this chapter. You can download the project from GitHub, delete the .git folder, and then check it in to TFVC.

We open a new build configuration just as we did earlier and follow these steps:

1. In the **General** tab, for **Build definition name**, enter Calc Api using Custom Build. We can leave the **Description** tab empty and leave **Queue processing** as **Enabled**.

2. We'll skip over the **Trigger** tab. This is because we want to leave the trigger as **Manual** so that this build isn't automatically run when there is a check-in of any new code.

3. Now, change the **Source Control Folder** tab in the **Active** row to include the Calc Api project, as shown here:

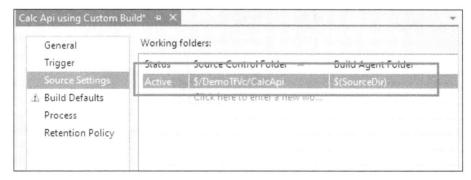

Figure 5: Source Settings

4. We'll remove **cloak** from the Drops folder because we are not pulling down the entire team projects source code, so not able to cloak that folder.

5. After that, we'll drop the builds into a UNC file share. For this to work, I created a share on my machine called Drops, as shown in the following screenshot, but you are welcome to use any UNC share:

Figure 6: The Drops shared folder

Make sure that your build agent has changed permissions on the UNC share. Otherwise, your build will fail.

6. In the **Build Defaults** tab, we are going to enter the full UNC path to where we want to place our drops, like this:

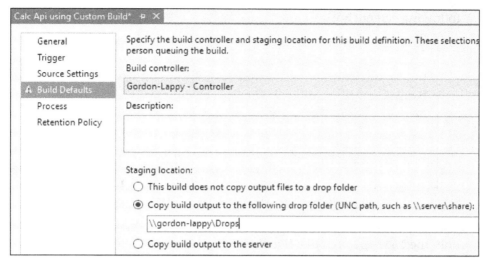

Figure 7: Setting the build drop location in Build Defaults

7. Next, go to the **Process** tab and then click on the **New...** button, as highlighted here:

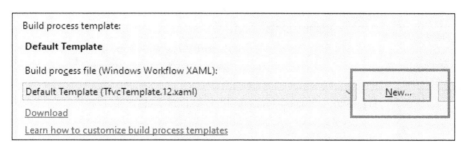

Figure 8: Adding a new build template

8. If you are using TFVC, then at this point, you can simply type the server path to `CustomTfvcTemplate.12.xaml`. Alternatively, click on **Browse**, navigate to `CustomTfvcTemplate.12.xaml`, and then click on **OK**, as shown in the following screenshot:

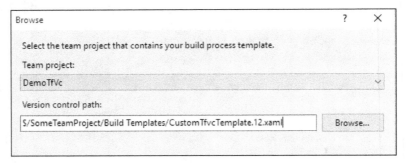

Figure 9: Browsing for a build template in a TFVC project

9. The only other thing we are going to set is **Projects**, in which we will select only the `CalcApi.sln` file, like this:

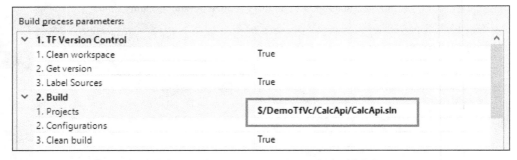

Figure 10: Setting the Projects property in the build definition

10. We don't need to change anything in the **Retention Policy** tab, so we can click on **Save**. You can now queue a new build, as shown in the following screenshot:

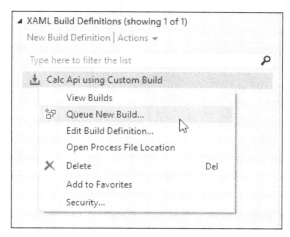

Figure 11: Queuing a new build

11. We'll leave all the defaults for the **Queue Build** dialog as they are and then click on **Queue**. This build should succeed with no issues.

Figure 12: Build completed successfully

Now that our build is set up and working, we can make modifications to the build template, and if the build fails without us changing the code, we know that it's our changes that are breaking the build.

Creating custom activities

A build definition is made up of a whole lot of components, called activities.
Let's start creating our own activity by creating a new **Activity Library**, as shown
in this screenshot:

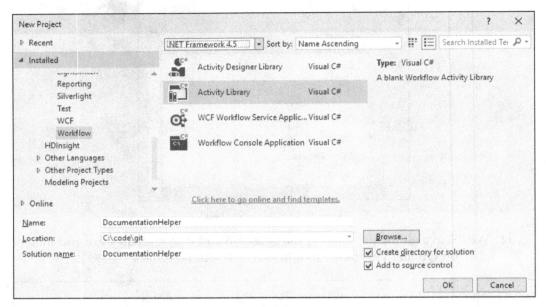

Figure 13: A new Activity Library project

First, let's delete the `Activity1.xaml` file that was created for us in the project.
Next, add a code activity called `DocumentBuildActivity.cs`. You will find the
Code Activity item template under the **Workflow** section in the **Add New Item**
dialog. Now, we need to add a reference to `Microsoft.TeamFoundation.Build.`
`Client.dll`. We are going to use `NuGet` for this package instead of searching for
our local machine as we did previously in this chapter.

There is a `NuGet` package that is now available for TFS 2015 and contains all the
object model assemblies in it. To do this, we will open **Package Manager Console**
in Visual Studio and then make sure that `http://www.nuget.org/` is set as the
package source. Your activities project is selected as the default project, and then
type this line:

```
Install-Package Microsoft.TeamFoundationServer.Client
```

When you press *Enter*, this will go to http://www.nuget.org/, get all the dependencies for this package, and install them for you.

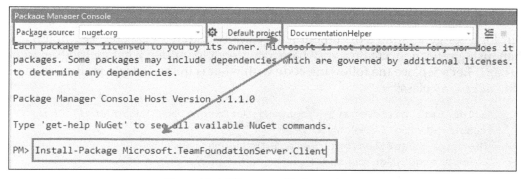

Figure 14: Adding a new NuGet package

Once you see the PM> line again, it means that everything has been installed. Now do the same thing for the extended client:

```
Install-Package Microsoft.TeamFoundationServer.ExtendedClient
```

This will install slightly more dependencies. Open your DocumentBuildActivity class and add the following attribute to it:

```
[BuildActivity(HostEnvironmentOption.Agent)]
```

Then add the using statement:

```
using Microsoft.TeamFoundation.Build.Client;
```

We add the BuildActivity attribute so that our activity is discoverable, and then we specify HostEnvironmentOption as **Agent** so as to inform TFS that the activity can run only on an agent.

Activity-specific logic

Now, we will start off with the logic that is specific to this activity, and this is what we are going to focus on.

Our logic for generating a document will basically search for specific assemblies and then, using reflection, create a very basic document to outline what methods exist in our api. Let's replace the following code with what is in the execute method in our code activity class:

```
IBuildDetail buildDetail = context.GetExtension<IBuildDetail>();
foreach (string filePath in
  Directory.GetFiles(buildDetail.DropLocation,
    DocsTarget.Get(context),
      SearchOption.AllDirectories))
{
  GenerateDocsFor(filePath);
}
```

Then, after the execute method, insert the following code:

```
[RequiredArgument]
public InArgument<string> DocsTarget { get; set; }
private void GenerateDocsFor(string filePath)
{
  throw new NotImplementedException();
}
```

Also add the using statement:

```
using System.IO;
```

We will then add some basic logic to the GenerateDocsFor method to scan the assembly with a name that is passed from the DocsTarget property, which we are saying is a required argument, and its type is string for an input. In the GenerateDocsFor method, place the following code:

```
var assem = Assembly.LoadFile(filePath);
string result = string.Empty;
foreach (var tCalss in assem.GetTypes().
  Where(o => o.IsClass))
{
  result += $"{tCalss.Name}\r\n";
  foreach (var method in tCalss.GetMethods())
  {
    result += $"\t{method.Name}\r\n";
```

```
    }
}
File.WriteAllText($"{filePath}.txt", result);
```

And add this `using` statement for reflection:

```
using System.Reflection;
```

We find everything that is matched by the input argument and then build a text file. Finally, we write a new file to the same location as the target, with `.txt` at the end.

How do I use a custom activity in a build template?

The easiest way to add an activity to a build definition is to actually have the build definition as part of the same solution. If you are using separate source controls for current build templates and your activities, then you can either move the build templates permanently into a solution file as an activity library, or keep copying the build template to your main project. For now, what I will do is move the build template and change the source in the build definition later. Add a new **Activity Library** project to the solution, as follows:

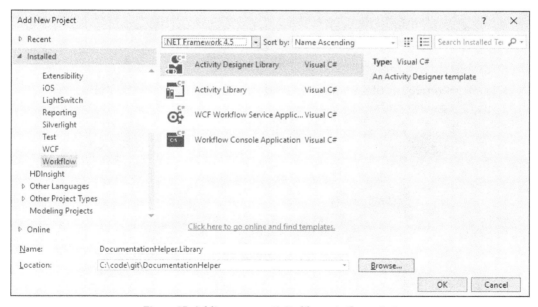

Figure 15: Adding a new activity library to the project

We delete the `ActivityDesigner1.xaml` file, which was automatically created for us, and then copy and paste the `CustomTfvcTemplate.12.xaml` file we saved earlier into this project. Set **Build Action** to **Content**. Now open your template file, and when all the workflow steps are collapsed, it should look something like this:

Figure 16: The build template workflow

Open the **Run on agent** block and then find the **Finally** block of the main `try`, `catch`, and `finally`, as shown here:

Figure 17: The Finally block for running on an agent

At this point, if you look at the toolbox, you will see that there is a new item for your activity, like this:

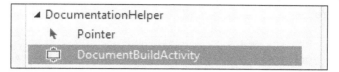

Figure 18: A custom build activity in the toolbox

Drag that item from the toolbox to just before the **Reset the Environment** block. The flow will now look like what is shown in the following screenshot:

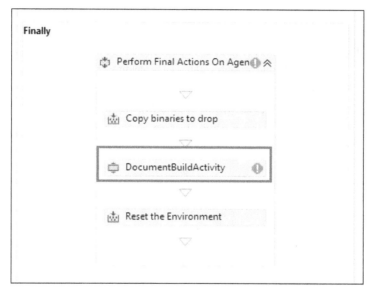

Figure 19: A new build activity in the build template

As you can see, there are now also exclamation marks in a couple of places. This is because there are required parameters that we have not yet filled in. Right-click on your new activity, click on **Properties**, and set the **DocsTarget** property to `CalcApi.dll`, as shown here:

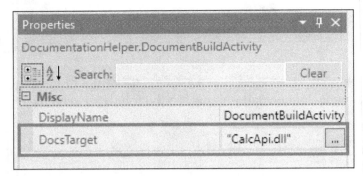

Figure 20: Setting the DocsTarget property

After saving, your build template will now know about your new activity, and all that is left to do is make TFS know about it as well. One way in which we can do this is by creating a folder called `CustomAssemblies` in the root of the current solution, above the `DocumentationHelper` and `DocumentationHelper.Library` folders, as shown in this screenshot:

	Name	Date modified	Type	Size
☐	.git	9/9/2015 8:29 PM	File folder	
	.vs	8/19/2015 5:31 PM	File folder	
☑	CustomAssemblies	8/19/2015 5:32 PM	File folder	
	DocumentationHelper	8/19/2015 5:32 PM	File folder	
	DocumentationHelper.Library	8/19/2015 5:32 PM	File folder	
	packages	8/19/2015 5:33 PM	File folder	
	.gitattributes	7/30/2015 11:26 PM	Text Document	3 KB
	.gitignore	7/30/2015 11:26 PM	Text Document	4 KB
	DocumentationHelper.sln	7/31/2015 12:34 AM	Microsoft Visual S...	2 KB

Figure 21: The CustomAssemblies folder

Now copy all the contents from the activity project's `bin` folder to the new folder you just created, add the files to the source control, and check in the changes. I know that this is not the best idea if you are using Git to check in binaries, and it's part of the reason I'd recommend using TFVC to store your build activities.

> With centralized source control (such as TFVC), when you get the latest version of the code, you are given the latest version of each file. Distributed source control (such as Git) works very differently; when you get the latest version of the code, you get the entire repository, with all its history. Keeping binaries in the source control is a bad practice anyway, but with distributed source control, I would say it's frowned upon even more. This is because each time you replace those files, an entirely new copy of the file will be moved around all the time to each user of the repository instead of just the latest copy.

Now what you need to do is configure the build controller to look at the new path for custom assemblies, open the **Build** page in **Team Explorer** in Visual Studio, click on **Actions**, and then click on **Manage Build Controllers...**, as shown in the following screenshot:

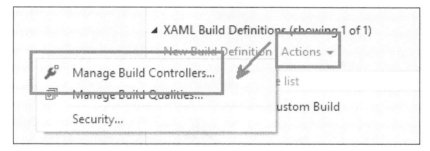

Figure 22: Manage Build Controllers

In the **Manage Build Controllers** window, click on **Properties....** Then, in the **Build Controllers Properties** window, click on **Browse by version control path to custom assemblies**. Next, just as with the process for using the custom build template, we fill in the dialog, but we use the CustomAssemblies folder, as shown in the following screenshot:

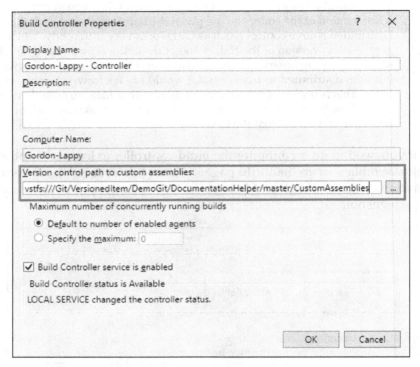

Figure 23: Setting the path to custom assemblies

Click **OK**, then on **OK** again, and then on **Close**. When you modify these values, the agents will automatically be updated with the new values, so you don't have to worry about going and restarting any agents yourself.

Remember to switch your build definition to use the new build template that you have included in your activities' project.

If you rerun your build now, you should see that it still succeeds, and if you go to the drops, you will see the doc file, like this:

Figure 24: The doc file that was generated as part of the build

If you look into this file, you will notice that the classes and all the properties are written in it.

You can see some community built components on GitHub at https://github.com/tfsbuildextensions/CustomActivities.

A walkthrough of the new build system

So, we've covered the old build system, and as you can see, there is quite a bit of effort involved in changing the way your build behaves. The new build system is a lot easier to set up, and all that you need to configure and administer your builds is your browser. It also has agents that are cross-platform, which is a huge advantage over the old build system.

To get started, go to the **BUILD** hub in the web access, and then click on the green add button, as marked here:

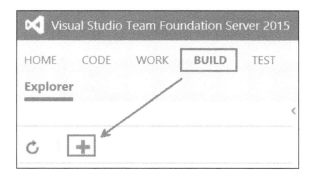

Figure 25: Opening a new definition templates dialog

This will then pop up a list of base **Build** and **Deployment** templates for you to start off with, as shown in the following screenshot:

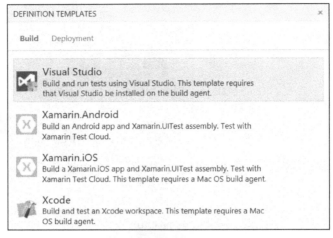

Figure 26: DEFINITION TEMPLATES

As you can see, there are templates for iOS and Android as well. We'll select **Visual Studio** for now and click on **OK**. You can also see that the default template has most of what you'd want to do with most builds, as follows:

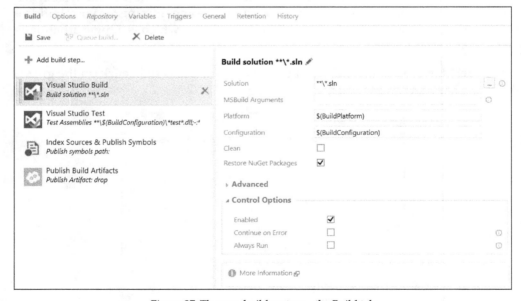

Figure 27: The new build system – the Build tab

By default, you get four build steps—**Build**, **Test**, **Index Symbols**, and **Publish**—but there are a lot of other build steps, from more complicated things, such as running load tests in Visual Studio Online, to simpler things, such as running a PowerShell script. Click on **Add build step...** to see a list of tasks that are available, as shown in this screenshot:

Figure 28: ADD BUILD STEPS

As you can see to the left, there are different categories (**Build**, **Utility**, **Test**, **Package**, and **Deploy**). You will also notice in the right-hand-side panel, under **Build** for example, that there are tasks for Maven, Gulp, Android, and iOS. From this dialog, you just have to click on **Add**. Then the task will be added to your definition, and you can configure any parameters that the build task exposes.

The **Visual Studio Build** step, which was added as part of our template, builds all the solution files that are found. Under the **Options** tab, you can select whether you want to run **Multiple Configurations**, like this:

Figure 29: The new build system – the Options tab

The **Repository** tab is where you select your source control. For TFVC, it's simple and feels very much like the old build system's UX.

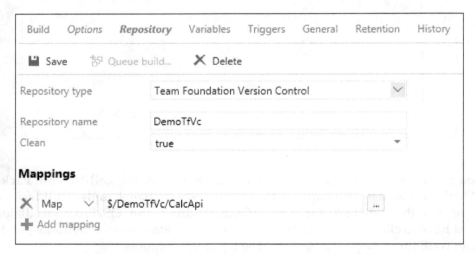

Figure 30: The new build system – the Repository tab (TFVC)

For Git in TFS, the UX is very simple, as shown here:

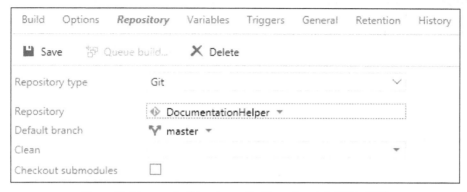

Figure 31: The new build system – the Repository tab (Git in TFS)

Now, the build system in both a TFVC project and a Git Team project has another option for **Repository Type**, which is **External Git**, as shown in the following screenshot:

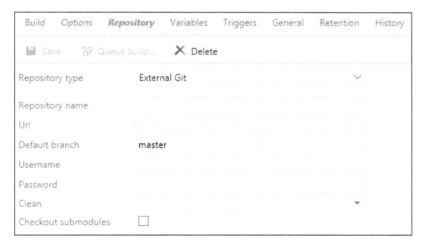

Figure 32: The new build system – the Repository tab (External Git)

This is very useful if you have code that is not hosted in TFS; maybe, the code is in GitHub, or it is hosted in another Team Project Collection. If you need to build such code, you don't have to go to a new place to do it. You can simply add the URL and credentials here, and you are all set! Then, if we take a look at the **Variables** tab, we can see all the variables that will be passed through to our build, like this:

Figure 33: The new build system – the Variables tab

Moving over to the **Triggers** tab, we can configure **Continuous Integration (CI)**, as shown in the following screenshot, and/or configure the running of our build on a schedule, such as nightly:

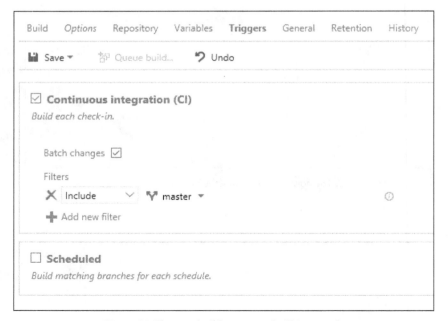

Figure 34: The new build system – the Triggers tab

Under CI, we are only given the option for batch builds at this point, and not many options. Under **Scheduled**, we can add all the times when we want the build to run as well as the days. Next, under the **General** tab, we are able to set the default queue (pool of agents) to be used for this build. We set some format for the build number and also set the demands that we have for the agent that will build our code. So, we can specify that the agent must have Visual Studio, .NET 4.6, and more. There is a nice post at `http://nakedalm.com/using-build-vnext-capabilities-demands-system/` by Martin Hinshelwood that explains the demands system.

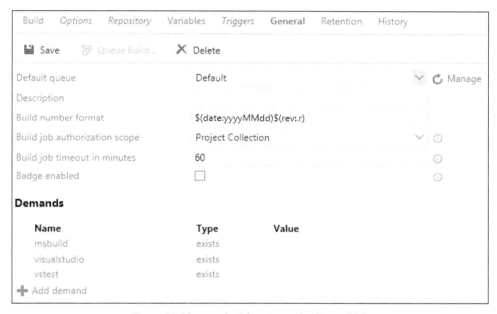

Figure 35: The new build system – the General tab

Next, we have the **Retention** tab. It's here that you can choose for how long you want to keep builds.

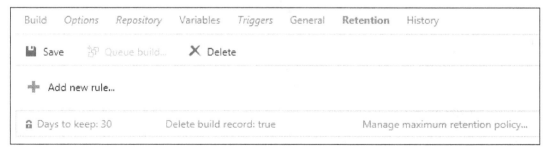

Figure 36: The new build system – The Retention tab

The last tab that we have is the **History** tab. Under this tab, you will be able to see all the changes that have been made to the build definition, as shown in the following screenshot:

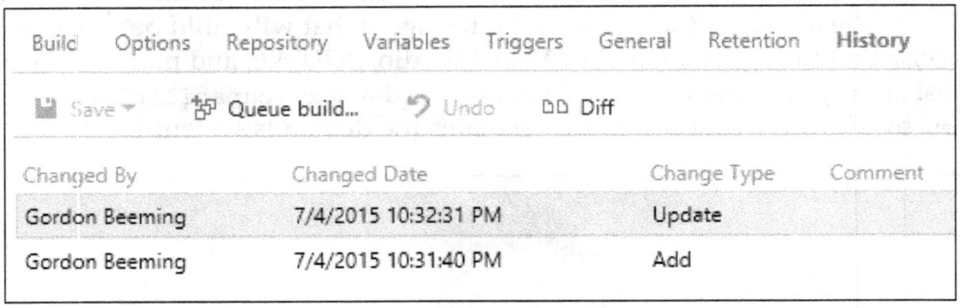

Figure 37 - The new Build System - the History tab

You are able to compare the changes from one version to the next under this tab, as illustrated here:

Figure 38: The new build system – the History tab with the Diff changes

Although you can see a great difference in the changes, it is good practice to insert a comment when you make those changes, so that people can easily understand what you did without only seeing raw changes and then trying to understand why you made them.

In conclusion, the new build system is better and faster and supports more than what we were used to with the old system. Another great thing about the new build system is that most of its parts are open source.

 Here are a few resources for build agents:

- **Agent**: `https://github.com/Microsoft/vso-agent`
- **Agent Tasks**: `https://github.com/Microsoft/vso-agent-tasks`
- **Agent Samples**: `https://github.com/Microsoft/vso-agent-samples`

If there is something that you think should be added, fork the repository, make your changes, and then submit a pull request. The concerned Microsoft product team will then review your pull requests and possibly merge your changes with the master branch, which will then be included in the product.

Summary

In this chapter, we took a look at what is required to create a new build activity and how we can use a new activity in builds. We then covered the new build system in TFS and took a walk through the set up of a new build.

In the next chapter, we will be taking a look at TFS scheduled jobs. We'll find out what they are, when they should be used, and when they shouldn't be used.

8
Creating TFS Scheduled Jobs

In this chapter, we are going to cover TFS scheduled jobs. The topics that we are going to cover include:

- Writing a TFS job
- Deploying a TFS job
- Removing a TFS job

You would want to write a scheduled job for any logic that needs to be run at specific times, whether it is at certain increments or at specific times of the day. A scheduled job is not the place to put logic that you would like to run as soon as some other event, such as a check-in or a work item change, occurs.

In our example, we'll create a TFS job that will be able to replace one of the examples we created in *Chapter 6, Enforcing Standards with Server-Side Plugins*. It will automatically link change sets to work items based on the comments.

The project setup

First off, we'll start with our project setup. This time, we'll create a Windows console application.

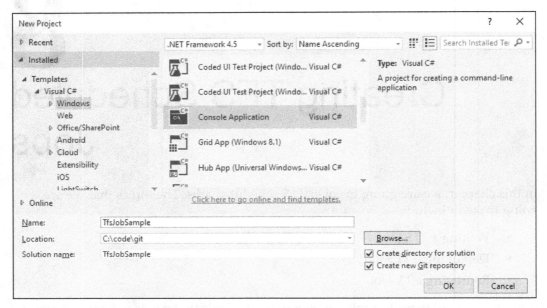

Creating a new Windows console application

The references that we'll need this time around are:

- `Microsoft.VisualStudio.Services.WebApi.dll`
- `Microsoft.TeamFoundation.Common.dll`
- `Microsoft.TeamFoundation.Framework.Server.dll`

All of these can be found in `C:\Program Files\Microsoft Team Foundation Server 14.0\Application Tier\TFSJobAgent` on the TFS server.

That's all the setup that is required for your TFS job project. Any class that inherits `ITeamFoundationJobExtension` will be able to be used for a TFS job.

Writing the TFS job

So, as mentioned, we are going to need a class that inherits from
ITeamFoundationJobExtension.

Let's create a class called TfsCommentsToChangeSetLinksJob and inherit from
ITeamFoundationJobExtension. As part of this, we will need to implement the
Run method, which is part of an interface, like this:

```
public class TfsCommentsToChangeSetLinksJob :
ITeamFoundationJobExtension
{
  public TeamFoundationJobExecutionResult Run(
      TeamFoundationRequestContext requestContext,
      TeamFoundationJobDefinition jobDefinition,
      DateTime queueTime, out string resultMessage)
  {
    throw new NotImplementedException();
  }
}
```

Then, we also add the using statement:

```
using Microsoft.TeamFoundation.Framework.Server;
```

Now, for this specific extension, we'll need to add references to the following:

* Microsoft.TeamFoundation.Client.dll
* Microsoft.TeamFoundation.VersionControl.Client.dll
* Microsoft.TeamFoundation.WorkItemTracking.Client.dll

All of these can be found in C:\Program Files\Microsoft Team Foundation
Server 14.0\Application Tier\TFSJobAgent.

Now, for the logic of our plugin, we use the following code inside of the Run method
as a basic shell, where we'll then place the specific logic for this plugin. This basic
shell will be adding a try catch block, and at the end of the try block, it will
return a successful job run. We'll then add to the job message what exception may be
thrown, returning that the job failed:

```
resultMessage = string.Empty;

try

{
```

```
    // place logic here


    return TeamFoundationJobExecutionResult.Succeeded;

}

catch (Exception ex)

{

    resultMessage += "Job Failed: " + ex.ToString();

    return TeamFoundationJobExecutionResult.Failed;

}
```

Along with this code, you will need the following `using` function:

```
using Microsoft.TeamFoundation;
using Microsoft.TeamFoundation.Client;
using Microsoft.TeamFoundation.VersionControl.Client;
using Microsoft.TeamFoundation.WorkItemTracking.Client;
using System.Linq;
using System.Text.RegularExpressions;
```

So next, we need to place some logic specific to this job in the `try` block. First, let's create a connection to TFS for version control:

```
TfsTeamProjectCollection tfsTPC =
        TfsTeamProjectCollectionFactory.GetTeamProjectCollection(
          new Uri("http://localhost:8080/tfs"));
VersionControlServer vcs =
        tfsTPC.GetService<VersionControlServer>();
```

Then, we will query the work item store's history and get the last 25 check-ins:

```
WorkItemStore wis = tfsTPC.GetService<WorkItemStore>();
// get the last 25 check ins
foreach (Changeset changeSet in vcs.QueryHistory("$/",
RecursionType.Full, 25))
{
    // place the next logic here
}
```

Now that we have the `changeset` history, we are going to check the comments for any references to work items using a simple `regex` expression:

```
//try match the regex for a hash number in the comment
foreach (Match match in Regex.Matches((changeSet.Comment
    ?? string.Empty), @"#\d{1,}"))
{
    // place the next logic here
}
```

Getting into this loop, we'll know that we have found a valid number in the comment and that we should attempt to link the check-in to that work item. But just the fact that we have found a number doesn't mean that the work item exists, so let's try to find a work item with the found number:

```
int workItemId = Convert.ToInt32(match.Value.TrimStart('#'));
var workItem = wis.GetWorkItem(workItemId);
if (workItem != null)
{
    // place the next logic here
}
```

Here, we are checking to make sure that the work item exists so that if the `workItem` variable is not null, then we'll proceed to check whether a relationship for this `changeSet` and `workItem` function already exists:

```
//now create the link
ExternalLink changesetLink = new ExternalLink(
wis.RegisteredLinkTypes[ArtifactLinkIds.Changeset],
changeSet.ArtifactUri.AbsoluteUri);
//you should verify if such a link already exists
if (!workItem.Links.OfType<ExternalLink>()
    .Any(l => l.LinkedArtifactUri ==
    changeSet.ArtifactUri.AbsoluteUri))
{
  // place the next logic here
}
```

If a link does not exist, then we can add a new link:

```
changesetLink.Comment = "Change set " +
        $"'{changeSet.ChangesetId}'" +
        " auto linked by a server plugin";
workItem.Links.Add(changesetLink);
workItem.Save();
resultMessage += $"Linked CS:{changeSet.ChangesetId} " +
                $"to WI:{workItem.Id}";
```

Most of this code logic sample is similar to that of the previous chapter; we just have the extra bit here so as to get the last 25 change sets. If you were using this for production, you would probably want to store the last change set that you processed and then get history up until that point, but I don't think it's needed to illustrate this sample.

Then, after getting the list of change sets, we basically process everything 100 percent as before. We check whether there is a comment and whether that comment contains a hash number that we can try linking to a `changeSet` function. We then check whether a `workItem` function exists for the number that we found. Next, we add a link to the work item from the `changeSet` function. Then, for each link we add to the overall `resultMessage` string so that when we look at the results from our job running, we can see which links were added automatically for us.

As you can see, with this approach, we don't interfere with the check-in itself but rather process this out-of-hand way of linking `changeSet` to work with items at a later stage.

Deploying our TFS job

Deploying the code is very simple; change the project's **Output type** to **Class Library**. This can be done by going to the project properties, and then in the **Application** tab, you will see an **Output type** drop-down list. Now, build your project. Then, copy the `TfsJobSample.dll` and `TfsJobSample.pdb` output files to the scheduled job plugins folder, which is `C:\Program Files\Microsoft Team Foundation Server 14.0\Application Tier\TFSJobAgent\Plugins`.

Unfortunately, simply copying the files into this folder won't make your scheduled job automatically installed, and the reason for this is that as part of the interface of the scheduled job, you don't specify when to run your job. Instead, you register the job as a separate step. Change **Output type** back to the **Console Application** option for the next step. You can, and should, split the TFS job from its installer into different projects, but in our sample, we'll use the same one.

Registering, queueing, and deregistering a TFS job

If you try to install the job the way you used to in TFS 2013, you will now get the TF400444 error:

TF400444: The creation and deletion of jobs is no longer supported. You may only update the EnabledState or Schedule of a job. Failed to create, delete or update job id 5a7a01e0-fff1-44ee-88c3-b33589d8d3b3

This is because they have made some changes to the job service, for security reasons, and these changes prevent you from using the **Client Object Model**. You are now forced to use the **Server Object Model**.

The code that you have to write is slightly more complicated and requires you to copy your executable to multiple locations to get it working properly. Place all of the following code in your `program.cs` file inside the `main` method.

We start off by getting some arguments that are passed through to the application, and if we don't get at least one argument, we don't continue:

```
#region Collect commands from the args
if (args.Length != 1 && args.Length != 2)
{
  Console.WriteLine("Usage: TfsJobSample.exe <command "+
                    "(/r, /i, /u, /q)> [job id]");
  return;
}
string command = args[0];
Guid jobid = Guid.Empty;
if (args.Length > 1)
{
  if (!Guid.TryParse(args[1], out jobid))
  {
    Console.WriteLine("Job Id not a valid Guid");
    return;
  }
}
#endregion
```

We then wrap all our logic in a `try` `catch` block, and for our `catch`, we only write the exception that occurred:

```
try
{
  // place logic here
}
catch (Exception ex)
{
  Console.WriteLine(ex.ToString());
}
```

Place the next steps inside the `try` block, unless asked to do otherwise. As part of using the Server Object Model, you'll need to create a `DeploymentServiceHost`. This requires you to have a connection string to the TFS Configuration database, so make sure that the connection string set in the following is valid for you. We also need some other generic path information, so we'll mimic what we could expect the job agents' paths to be:

```
#region Build a DeploymentServiceHost
string databaseServerDnsName = "localhost";
string connectionString = $"Data Source={databaseServerDnsName};"+
"Initial Catalog=TFS_Configuration;Integrated Security=true;";
TeamFoundationServiceHostProperties deploymentHostProperties =
    new TeamFoundationServiceHostProperties();
deploymentHostProperties.HostType =
            TeamFoundationHostType.Deployment |
            TeamFoundationHostType.Application;
deploymentHostProperties.Id = Guid.Empty;
deploymentHostProperties.PhysicalDirectory =
    @"C:\Program Files\Microsoft Team Foundation Server 14.0\"+
    @"Application Tier\TFSJobAgent";
deploymentHostProperties.PlugInDirectory =
    $@"{deploymentHostProperties.PhysicalDirectory}\Plugins";
deploymentHostProperties.VirtualDirectory = "/";
ISqlConnectionInfo connInfo =
    SqlConnectionInfoFactory.Create(connectionString,
                                    null, null);
DeploymentServiceHost host =
    new DeploymentServiceHost(deploymentHostProperties,
                                    connInfo, true);
#endregion
```

Now that we have a `TeamFoundationServiceHost` function, we are able to create a `TeamFoundationRequestContext` function. We'll need it to call methods such as `UpdateJobDefinitions`, which adds and/or removes our job, and `QueryJobDefinition`, which is used to queue our job outside of any schedule:

```
using (TeamFoundationRequestContext requestContext =
                               host.CreateSystemContext())
{
  TeamFoundationJobService jobService =
      requestContext.GetService<TeamFoundationJobService>()
  // place next logic here
}
```

We then create a new `TeamFoundationJobDefinition` instance with all of the information that we want for our TFS job, including the name, schedule, and enabled state:

```
var jobDefinition =
    new TeamFoundationJobDefinition(
            "Comments to Change Set Links Job",
            "TfsJobSample.TfsCommentsToChangeSetLinksJob");
jobDefinition.EnabledState =
    TeamFoundationJobEnabledState.Enabled;
jobDefinition.Schedule.Add(new TeamFoundationJobSchedule
{
  ScheduledTime = DateTime.Now,
  PriorityLevel = JobPriorityLevel.Normal,
  Interval = 300,
});
```

Once we have the job definition, we check what the command was and then execute the code that will relate to that command. For the `/r` command, we will just run our TFS job outside of the TFS job agent:

```
if (command == "/r")
{
  string resultMessage;
  new TfsCommentsToChangeSetLinksJob().Run(requestContext,
                  jobDefinition, DateTime.Now, out resultMessage);
}
```

For the `/i` command, we will install the TFS job:

```
else if (command == "/i")
{
  jobService.UpdateJobDefinitions(requestContext, null,
    new[] { jobDefinition });
}
```

For the `/u` command, we will uninstall the TFS job:

```
else if (command == "/u")
{
  jobService.UpdateJobDefinitions(requestContext,
    new[] { jobid }, null);
}
```

Finally, with the `/q` command, we will queue the TFS job to be run inside the TFS job agent and outside of its schedule:

```
else if (command == "/q")
{
  jobService.QueryJobDefinition(requestContext, jobid);
}
```

Now that we have this code in the `program.cs` file, we need to compile the project and then copy `TfsJobSample.exe` and `TfsJobSample.pdb` to the TFS `Tools` folder, which is `C:\Program Files\Microsoft Team Foundation Server 14.0\Tools`. Now open a `cmd` window as an administrator. Change the directory to the `Tools` folder and then run your application with a `/i` command, as follows:

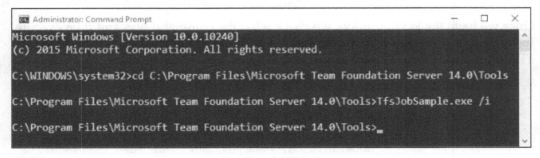

Installing the TFS job

Now, you have successfully installed the TFS job. To uninstall it or force it to be queued, you will need the job ID, which you will see how to get later in this chapter. But basically you have to run /u with the job ID to uninstall, like this:

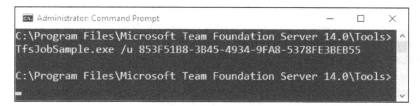

Uninstalling the TFS job

You will be following the same approach as prior for queuing, simply specifying the /q command and the job ID.

How do I know whether my TFS job is running?

The easiest way to check whether your TFS job is running or not is to check out the job history table in the configuration database. To do this, you will need the job ID (we spoke about this earlier), which you can obtain by running the following query against the TFS_Configuration database:

```
SELECT JobId
FROM Tfs_Configuration.dbo.tbl_JobDefinition WITH ( NOLOCK )
WHERE JobName = 'Comments to Change Set Links Job'
```

With this JobId, we will then run the following lines to query the job history:

```
SElECT *
FROM Tfs_Configuration.dbo.tbl_JobHistory WITH (NOLOCK)
WHERE JobId = '<place the JobId from previous query here>'
```

This will return you a list of results about the previous times the job was run. If you see that your job has a Result of 6 which is *extension not found*, then you will need to stop and restart the TFS job agent. You can do this by running the following commands in an Administrator cmd window:

```
net stop TfsJobAgent
net start TfsJobAgent
```

Note that when you stop the TFS job agent, any jobs that are currently running will be terminated. Also, they will not get a chance to save their state, which, depending on how they were written, could lead to some unexpected situations when they start again.

After the agent has started again, you will see that the Result field is now different as it is a job agent that will know about your job. If you prefer browsing the web to see the status of your jobs, you can browse to the job monitoring page (_oi/_jobMonitoring#_a=history), for example, http://gordon-lappy:8080/tfs/_oi/_jobMonitoring#_a=history. This will give you all the data that you can normally query but with nice graphs and grids.

Summary

In this chapter, we looked at how to write, install, uninstall, and queue a TFS job. You learned that the way we used to install TFS jobs will no longer work for TFS 2015 because of a change in the Client Object Model for security.

In this next chapter, we will be taking a look at service hooks in TFS and what you can use them for.

9
Service Hooks

Service hooks are a great way to keep your team up to date when they are disconnected from TFS or keep your communities up to date with the progress on your projects. Service hooks provide a mechanism to interact with external systems.

In this chapter, we will be taking a look at service hooks in TFS. The topics that we'll cover include the following:

- What service hooks are available?
- Why would you want to use service hooks?
- How can you use service hooks in TFS?

What service hooks are available?

TFS has several extremely useful service hooks available out of the box, including the following integrations (descriptions taken from TFS):

- **Azure Service Bus**: Microsoft Azure Service Bus provides a hosted, secure, and widely available infrastructure for widespread communication, large-scale event distribution, naming, and service publishing.
- **Azure Storage**: Microsoft Azure Storage is a service for storing large numbers of messages that can be accessed from anywhere in the world. It is useful for creating a backlog of work to process.
- **Bamboo**: Bamboo is a continuous integration server from Atlassian.

- **Campfire**: Campfire provides team collaboration with real-time chat. It is like instant messaging but is designed exclusively for groups.

- **Flowdock**: Flowdock provides chat and inbox for teams, providing one place to talk and stay up to date.

- **HipChat**: HipChat, from Atlassian, provides group chat and video chat built for teams.

- **Jenkins**: Jenkins is an open source continuous integration service popular with Java teams.

- **Kato**: Kato is a powerful collaboration platform based on simple chat that helps organizations move faster by decreasing their e-mail volume and making all communication instantly searchable.

- **Slack**: Slack is a searchable platform for team communication.

- **Trello**: Provides integration with Trello.

- **Web Hooks**: This provides event communication via HTTP.

- **Zendesk**: Zendesk is an SaaS suite that offers help desk ticketing, issue tracking, and customer service support.

If this list doesn't have something that you use for your team, there are a couple of others available that you can see using `https://www.visualstudio.com/get-started/integrate/integrating-with-service-hooks-vs`. Each of these service hooks has different types of events that can be used in each system, such as build, code, and work item events.

Why would you want to use service hooks?

As already mentioned, you would want to use service hooks to help keep your team members updated on certain events that are happening in TFS when they aren't connected. For this type of integration, lots of teams can and do use a service such as slack to stay updated for when builds fail and new commits are made for source repos that they care about.

Another use is when you want to keep your community updated with the status of your project, whether it is updating a publicly visible Trello board or maybe something like integrating with User Voice.

The other occasion when you may want to use service hooks is if you want to integrate with another system that is part of your release and deployment pipeline, for example, using a service such as MyGet.

How can you use service hooks in TFS?

To get started with integration with TFS, you will need to navigate to the **Service Hooks** tab in the admin section of a specific team project. Service hooks are configured per team project. To get this option, click on the little settings icon when you have a team project open, as shown in the following screenshot, and then click on the **Service Hooks** tab. Next, you need to create a new subscription; to do this, click on **Create the first subscription for this project**, as follows:

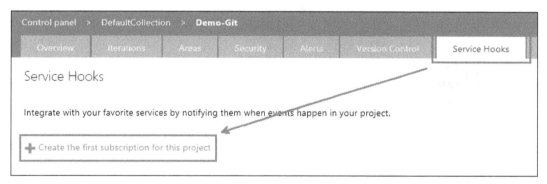

Figure 1: The Service Hooks tab in admin

This will bring forth the **NEW SERVICE HOOKS SUBSCRIPTION** dialog. This dialog will list everything that we mentioned earlier in this chapter under the *What service hooks are available?* section. We are going to integrate with Trello for our example, so we select **Trello** from the pane on the left, as shown in this screenshot:

Figure 2: NEW SERVICE HOOKS SUBSCRIPTION – The Service step

In the right-hand-side pane, you can see the supported actions and events that are available for Trello. Each service integration also has a link at the bottom that you can click on to learn more about that specific integration. Click on **Next** to go to the **Trigger** step, as shown here:

Figure 3: NEW SERVICE HOOKS SUBSCRIPTION – The Trigger step

For the **Trigger on this type of event** option, select **Work item created**. In the **FILTERS** field, select **Area path** and **Work item type,** and then click on **Next** to select the action details. Upon clicking, the following dialog box will open:

Figure 4: NEW SERVICE HOOKS SUBSCRIPTION – The Action step

In the **Action** step, we will need to provide some parameters that will be used to create a new card in Trello. Let's start off by getting a new user token. To do this, click on the **Get it now** link and allow VSO (or in this case, TFS) to integrate with Trello. You will be asked to sign in if you haven't already:

Figure 5: Allowing VSO to integrate with Trello

After you have allowed your VSO to integrate with Trello, you should be taken to a page that gives you a user token, like this:

You have granted access to your Trello information.

To complete the process, please give this token:

0b1633f45120e03c32c4fac1804bad7babc7dc4f867ef543c9679de0bdc38861

Figure 6: A user token from Trello

Place the token in the **User token** field. If the token is entered correctly, you will see a little tick next to the field, as depicted in the following screenshot:

Figure 7: The input field showing a valid input

With our user token supplied, the **Board** drop-down list will be populated from Trello. Once you have selected a board, you will see that the **List** field is loaded, and you can choose which list you want to create the new card in. You can also choose a value for the labels if you want, which we'll leave blank. Then, you are given the option of creating new cards at the top of the list or leaving them at the bottom of the list. We'll leave this unchecked for now:

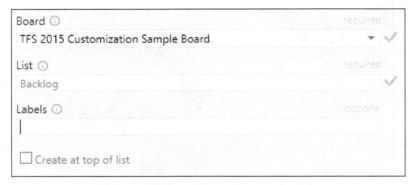

Figure 8: The input for Board, List, and Labels

The last things left that we can fill in are the card name and description. These default to the **System.Title** and **System.Description** (or equivalent) options of the work item created in TFS, which is fine for now. If you want to see what options can be put into those fields, you can click on the **Supports template** link.

Completing and verifying the service hook works

To complete this process, you can click on **Finish**, but let's click on **Test** first to see whether it works. If everything works the way it should, you will see the result as shown in this screenshot:

Figure 9: The TEST NOTIFICATION dialog

From this dialog, you are able to take a look at the JSON request and response in the other tabs in the dialog. After we have run the test, we will have a card created for us in Trello with the details that showed up on the test dialog, as shown in the following screenshot:

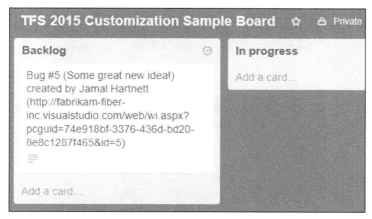

Figure 10: A test item created for us in Trello

You can go ahead and archive this card in Trello, because I'm sure you won't need it. Click on **Close** on the **Test** dialog, and then click on **Finish** on the original dialog. You should now see your service hook subscription showing up in a grid, as depicted in this screenshot:

Figure 11: Configured Service Hooks

You can click on the little arrow on the left-hand side to disable the service hook, edit some of its configuration, or delete it, like this:

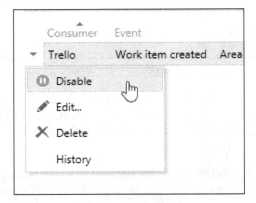

Figure 12: The Service Hook Subscription context menu

You also have similar options available above the grid and the option of **HISTORY**, which shows you all the events and actions triggered and their status, as follows:

Figure 13: The HISTORY dialog for a Service Hook Subscription

Suppose you created your trigger the same way as shown earlier for any area path and for the PBIs. Then, if you create a new PBI, you should see it in the **History** tab and also in the **Trello** option under the list you specified.

Summary

In this chapter, we looked at what service hooks are and what you can use them for. We then took a detailed look at how to create a new service hook for Trello, where we configured all newly created PBI work items for publishing on Trello.

In the next chapter, we will step out of TFS and move on to VSO to look at the new extension model that we will, hopefully, soon be seeing in TFS on premise.

10
VSO Extensions

In this chapter, we will be focusing on a topic that is not related to mainstream TFS activities but will hopefully be soon. We will be discussing **VSO Extensions** and some of its important aspects, including the following:

- What is VSO Extensions?
- Why should I invest time in this extension model?
- How do I build my own extension?

At the time of writing this book, this new extension model is available in VSO only, and it is a private beta version that you are able to get access to if you are part of the Microsoft Industry Partner Program (https://vsipprogram.com/).

What is VSO Extensions?

VSO Extensions is the new UI extension model that is being used for web access. It allows us to create custom supported extensions throughout the web access. This includes extending areas such as menus and toolbars into the following hubs:

- Build
- Code
- Test
- Work

You can also create your own hubs and hub groups if you want, and then build a complete app UI embedded inside TFS for applications such as the TFS time tracker (http://www.tfs-timetracker.com/).

VSO Extensions is, as a single package, called an extension, and then inside each extension are one or more contributions. These contributions can be all the core TFS contributions, or they can be contributions exposed from your own extension or other extensions.

The extensions are mostly HTML and JavaScript with an extension manifest file that has metadata about the extension presented as JSON. For security purposes, the content for these extensions needs to be hosted using HTTPS. This isn't a problem for small and community-type projects because you can host them on Azure, for which you get free SSL hosting even with the free sites. This can be done by simply changing `http` to `https` on any of your freely hosted sites, which is shown at `https://binary-stuff.com/post/a-hello-world-for-vso-extensions`.

Why invest time in this extension model?

In the past, we were able to create plugins for web accesses such as Tiago Pascoal's Task Board Enhancer (`http://pascoal.net/task-board-enhancer/`). In essence, if you read Team Foundation Server 2013 Customization (`http://bit.ly/MX0yVb`), you will remember that we mentioned that the old way of creating these kinds of plugins is not supported by Microsoft. As new updates are released for TFS on premise, you could spend quite a lot of time refiguring out the APIs, as they can and do change as required by the product. You have to consider that has a risk when delving into that extension model.

With this new model, it is completely supported by Microsoft, so you can expect similar compatibility as you have today with Visual Studio and the client object model that Microsoft ships. This makes the model a lot more attractive, as you know that the time to update plugins will not be the reason to stay on older versions of TFS.

The other great reason for investing time in the new extension model is that it is really simple to do and requires very little code for what before was hundreds of lines of scripts, depending on where you wanted to extend.

How do I build my own extension?

To continue with this section, you will need to be registered for VSO Extensions and have a publisher ID with which you have permissions to publish set up (`https://www.visualstudio.com/integrate/extensions/publish/overview`).

I usually use Visual Studio or Visual Studio Code to develop VSO Extensions. However, you can use any other editor if you want to. Visual Studio is the preferred way of creating these extensions for me at least:

- I mostly use TypeScript, which works nicely in Visual Studio, instead of raw JavaScript
- Visual Studio also easily configures SSL in IIS Express for you, which is a requirement for VSO Extensions

A new empty web application is usually a good starting point for one of these projects. The other option is to use the Visual Studio template by Josh Garverick (`https://visualstudiogallery.msdn.microsoft.com/a00f6cfc-4dbb-4b9a-a1b8-4d24bf46770b`). It does what is explained as follows. When you have created a new empty web application project, go to the properties for the web application project and you will see a property called **SSL Enabled**. Change its value to **true** and then make a note of the SSL URL, as shown here:

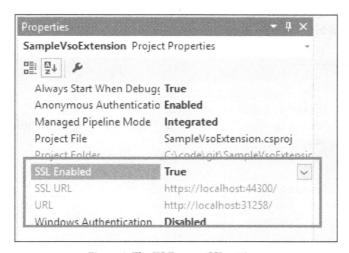

Figure 1: The IIS Express SSL settings

You will need this SSL URL for your extension manifest.

The extension manifest – content and SDK

The extension manifest is what contains all of the information for your extension—information on what contributions your extension uses as well as where the content needs to be loaded for those contributions.

The manifest file is used so that VSO knows which file contains the meta info required. Let's create a new file called `vss-extension.json` for our extension:

```
{
    "manifestVersion": 1,
    "id": "sample-ticker",
    "version": "0.1.0",
    "name": "Ticker (Sample)",
    "description": "Shows the current time.",
    "baseUri": "https://localhost:44300/",
    "publisher": "gordon-beeming",
    "icons": {
        "default": "images/logo.png"
    },
    "tags": [
        "Sample"
    ],
    "categories": [
        "Productivity"
    ],
    "contributions": [
        {
            "id": "Samples.Tickker",
            "type": "ms.vss-web.hub",
            "description": "'Ticker' hub on the Home hub group.",
            "targets": [
                "ms.vss-web.home-hub-group"
            ],
            "properties": {
                "name": "Ticker",
                "order": 99,
                "uri": "index.html"
            }
        }
    ]
}
```

What we have basically done here is set up some very basic metadata with information, such as the name, description, publisher (which you will need to change to your publisher ID), and categories of our extension. Then, we specified the contribution that is a new hub group on the home hub. We also specified the icon that should be used for our application when it is displayed in the marketplace. You can place an `icon.png` file in an `images` folder in your project for this.

More information about the extension manifest can be found at `https://www.visualstudio.com/en-us/integrate/extensions/develop/manifest`.

As part of the properties for the contribution, we specify that we will be loading in a page called `index.html`, which will come off what we set as `baseUrl`. You should update to the SSL URL in your project properties. Let's create the `index.html` page, which will have all the content for our simple extension:

```html
<html>
<head>
    <title>Ticker</title>
</head>
<body>
    <h1>Time</h1>
    <p id="ticker"></p>
    <script>
        setInterval(function () {
            document.getElementById("ticker").innerHTML
                = new Date();
        }, 1000);
    </script>
</body>
</html>
```

The logic in this page just sets the value of an `html` element on a 1-second interval to the current date.

Next up, we need to add a reference to the VSS SDK, which can be found on GitHub (`https://github.com/Microsoft/vso-extension-samples/blob/master/build-inspector/sdk/scripts/VSS.SDK.js`). Download this file and place it in a `scripts` folder in your project.

Packaging and publishing on the marketplace

In order to package your extension, you will need to download and install Node.js (`https://nodejs.org/`). Also, while going through the installer, make sure you have the add to **PATH** option selected.

After the installation is complete, open a new `cmd` window and install the VSO Extension Tool with the following command line:

```
npm i -g vset
```

Next, you will need a personal access token from VSO. Navigate to `https://<your account>.visualstudio.com/_details/security/tokens`. Click on **Add** and then you will be presented with a form, as shown in the following screenshot. In the form, you need to specify the **Description** field. You can leave the **Expires In** field for the token as **90 days** and change the **Accounts** field to **All accessible accounts**:

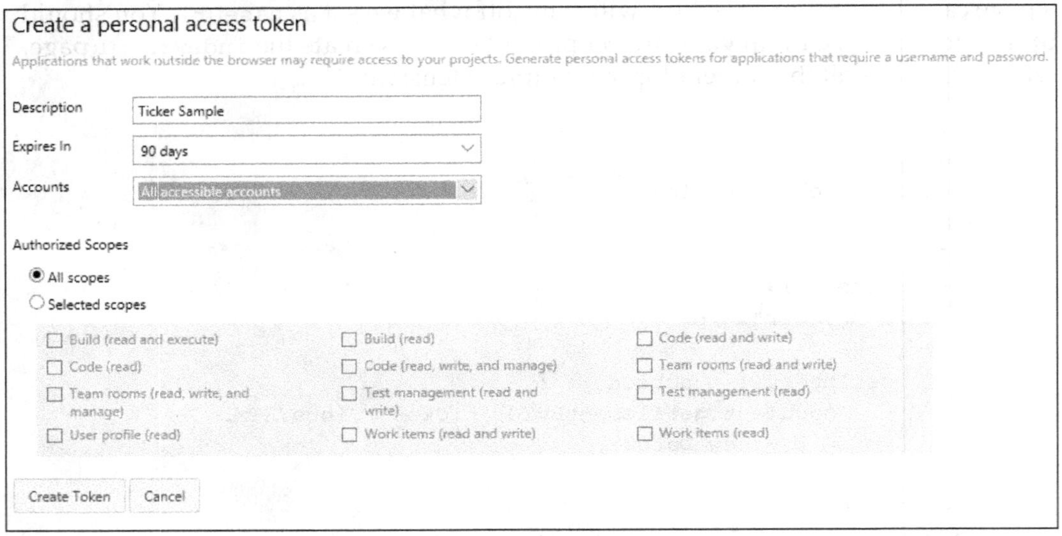

Figure 2: VSO – Create a personal access token

After you've clicked on **Create Token**, you will be shown your access token. Make sure you copy it out of this page as there is no way to retrieve the token once you navigate away from this page.

Next, we will use the `vset` tool we installed to package our extension. We can do this using the following command. Remember to change the directory in your Command Prompt to where your extension project is and also replace the following token with your token:

```
vset publish --output-path output --token
4fus7ekzf7okmakqnqtmmjdlphqomczx6he4szfexfat9ykcgmua
```

If all goes well—and it should—you will get a response similar to the one shown in the following screenshot:

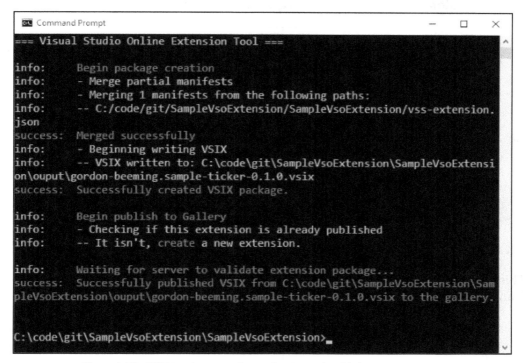

Figure 3: The VSET tool output after packaging and publishing an extension

Now, if you browse to your account in the VSO Market (`https://app.market.visualstudio.com/manage`), you will see that your extension has been published, like this:

Figure 4: The extension appearing in the VSO Market after publishing

Your extension is now in the VSO Market, and you can now share it with other accounts so that they are able to use it. To do this, click on the little arrow to left of the extension and then click on **Share**, as shown here:

Figure 5: The Extension context menu

This will pop up a dialog. Here, you can type the account name of any account you want to share your extension with, like this:

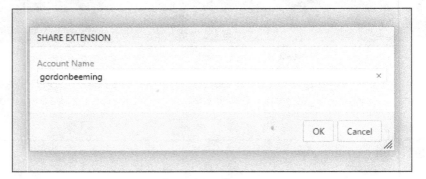

Figure 6: The SHARE EXTENSION dialog

Now, the admin of that account is able to go to the **Extensions** tab
(`https://<your account>.visualstudio.com/_admin/_apps/hub/ms.vss-extensionManagement-web.manageExtensions`) in the TFS Web Access **Control panel** and enable that extension in that account, as shown in the following screenshot:

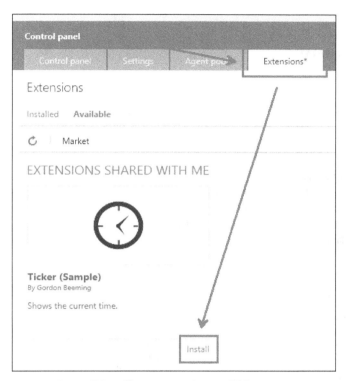

Figure 7: Installing an extension in a VSO account

Once you click on **Install**, the extension will be installed in the account. You will then be shown the **Uninstall** and **Disable the extension** links instead of the **Install** link.

If you browse to the home hub, you will see the **Ticker** hub group you created, as follows:

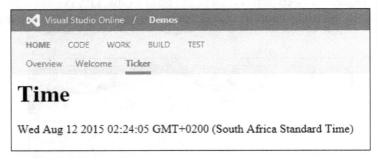

Figure 8: A new extension running in VSO

As you can see, everything is running as expected.

That's all that is required for creating a VSO extension. As you can see, it is really simple to get going. The process that we just followed had a lot of manual steps in it. However, we must remember that this system is still in beta and these components are still being built. Each deployment brings with it more major updates in the way we interact with VSO Extensions.

How can I stay up to date with VSO Extensions?

There are a couple of ways by which you can stay up to date with VSO Extensions. The easiest would probably be to follow feeds, blogs, and code repos. In the following sections, we will expound some aspects of staying up to date with VSO Extensions.

The extensions for the VSO site

The extensions for the Visual Studio Online site is probably the best place to get information from (https://www.visualstudio.com/en-us/integrate/extensions/overview) – directly from the product team of VSO Extensions. Also, a good place to keep a close eye on would be the overview page (at the following link) and the release notes that inaugurate new releases and features from time to time:

- The **Overview** page, https://www.visualstudio.com/en-us/integrate/extensions/overview

- The **Release notes**, https://www.visualstudio.com/integrate/extensions/support/release-notes

On this site, there is also a link to another very valuable resource called VSO Extensions Samples. It has an example of nearly every type of contribution point that is currently supported, and it can be found on GitHub (`https://github.com/Microsoft/vso-extension-samples`).

ALM Rangers Community Extensions

The Microsoft Visual Studio ALM Rangers have also worked on a couple of extensions with which you can view samples of how to build VSO Extensions. You can also contribute to the extensions that already exist and you might find useful but maybe want to add a bit of functionality to. The best way of seeing a complete list of these extensions would be to search in the ALM Rangers GitHub account for VSO-Extensions (`https://github.com/ALM-Rangers?utf8=%E2%9C%93&query=VSO-Extension`). You can read more about the first ALM Rangers extensions by Wouter de Kort and what went into it on the ALM Rangers blog (`http://blogs.msdn.com/b/visualstudioalmrangers/archive/2015/07/02/folder-management-visual-studio-online-extension-by-wouter-de-kort.aspx`).

My blog

Another useful place to keep an eye on for VSO Extensions-related posts is my blog, where I not only show working extensions but also cover some of the pain points that I come across with them, at `https://binary-stuff.com/list/vso+extensions`.

If you keep an eye out, you will not miss a thing for VSO Extensions and will be able to get the most out of this great extensibility model.

Summary

In this chapter, we had an overview of VSO Extensions, what they are, why you would want to use them, and how they are beneficial over the old, unsupported way of creating plugins for web access. We also took a look at creating a new extension, from developing it to publishing it on the store.

Index

W

web control, creating for web access
  about 81
  code, for custom control 81-83
  custom control, debugging 84
  custom control, deploying 84
welcome pages 12
Windows Forms Control
  creating, for client applications 71
Windows SharePoint Services 51, 52
Work In Progress (WIP) 28
work item query charts
  pinning 4-7
work item query counts
  pinning, to dashboard 3, 4
work item query data
  pinning 3
Work Item Query Language (WIQL) 3
work items
  exporting 59
  importing 59

WorkItem Tracking folder
  about 52
  Categories.xml file 62
  LinkTypes 53
  process folder 59-61
  queries folder 54
  reference links 58
  TypeDefinitions 55

X

XAML build template
  about 117, 118
  downloading 118-120

Z

Zendesk 158

Thank you for buying
Team Foundation Server 2015 Customization

About Packt Publishing

Packt, pronounced 'packed', published its first book, *Mastering phpMyAdmin for Effective MySQL Management*, in April 2004, and subsequently continued to specialize in publishing highly focused books on specific technologies and solutions.

Our books and publications share the experiences of your fellow IT professionals in adapting and customizing today's systems, applications, and frameworks. Our solution-based books give you the knowledge and power to customize the software and technologies you're using to get the job done. Packt books are more specific and less general than the IT books you have seen in the past. Our unique business model allows us to bring you more focused information, giving you more of what you need to know, and less of what you don't.

Packt is a modern yet unique publishing company that focuses on producing quality, cutting-edge books for communities of developers, administrators, and newbies alike. For more information, please visit our website at www.packtpub.com.

About Packt Enterprise

In 2010, Packt launched two new brands, Packt Enterprise and Packt Open Source, in order to continue its focus on specialization. This book is part of the Packt Enterprise brand, home to books published on enterprise software – software created by major vendors, including (but not limited to) IBM, Microsoft, and Oracle, often for use in other corporations. Its titles will offer information relevant to a range of users of this software, including administrators, developers, architects, and end users.

Writing for Packt

We welcome all inquiries from people who are interested in authoring. Book proposals should be sent to author@packtpub.com. If your book idea is still at an early stage and you would like to discuss it first before writing a formal book proposal, then please contact us; one of our commissioning editors will get in touch with you.

We're not just looking for published authors; if you have strong technical skills but no writing experience, our experienced editors can help you develop a writing career, or simply get some additional reward for your expertise.

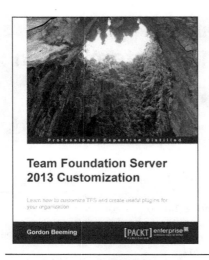

Team Foundation Server 2013 Customization

ISBN: 978-1-78217-714-2   Paperback: 102 pages

Learn how to customize TFS and create useful plugins for your organization

1. This book accelerates the understanding of TFS extension points.

2. Learn how to create a JavaScript web access plugin.

3. Discover the tips and tricks of customizing TFS.

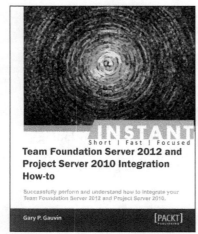

Instant Team Foundation Server 2012 and Project Server 2010 Integration How-to

ISBN: 978-1-84968-854-3   Paperback: 54 pages

Successfully perform and understand how to integrate your Team Foundation Server 2012 and Project Server 2010

1. Learn something new in an Instant! A short, fast, focused guide delivering immediate results.

2. Learn to plan and successfully implement your Team Foundation Server and Project Server integration.

3. Easily install or upgrade your Team Foundation Server extensions for Project Server.

Please check **www.PacktPub.com** for information on our titles

Team Foundation Server 2012 Starter

ISBN: 978-1-84968-838-3   Paperback: 72 pages

Your quick start guide to TFS 2012, top features, and best practices with hands on examples

1. Learn something new in an Instant! A short, fast, focused guide delivering immediate results.

2. Install TFS 2012 from scratch.

3. Get up and running with your first project.

Microsoft BizTalk Server 2010 Patterns

ISBN: 978-1-84968-460-6   Paperback: 396 pages

Create effective, scalable solutions with Microsoft BizTalk Server 2010

1. Provides a unified example from the beginning to end of a real world solution.

2. A starter guide expecting little or no previous BizTalk experience, but offering advanced concepts and techniques.

3. Provides in-depth background and introduction to the platform and technology.

Please check **www.PacktPub.com** for information on our titles

www.ingramcontent.com/pod-product-compliance
Lightning Source LLC
Chambersburg PA
CBHW060559060326
40690CB00017B/3760